Night Moves

THE SCIENCE OF MAKING HIM FALL IN LOVE WITH YOU

By Gregg Michaelsen

Copyright © 2017 Gregg Michaelsen and Confidence Builder LLC.

ISBN: 978-1-9798-4574-8

All rights reserved. No part of this publication may be reproduced, stored in a retrieval system, or transmitted in any form or by any means, electronic, mechanical, photocopying, recording, or otherwise, without written permission of the publisher.

DISCLAIMER: As a male dating coach I am very good at what I do because of my years of studying the nuances of interpersonal relationships. I have helped thousands of women understand men. That said, I am not a psychologist, doctor or licensed professional. So do not use my advice as a substitute if you need professional help.

Women tell me how much I have helped them and I truly hope that I can HELP you too in your pursuit of that extraordinary man! I will provide you with powerful tools. YOU need to bring me your willingness to listen and CHANGE!

Contents

INTRODUCTION: Can You Really Make Someone Fall in Love With You? 1
    Gregg, What About Love at First Sight? . . 2
    Okay so How Then? 3

CHAPTER 1: We're All Just a Bunch of Soybeans . . . 5
    Wrapping Up 9

CHAPTER 2: You Never Get a Second Chance to Make a First Impression 11
    Men are Visual 12
    What is Attractive? 14
    What Else do Men "Look" At? 15
    How do You Know? 17
    What's a Girl to Do? 18
    Wrapping Up 19

CHAPTER 3: Firing the First Shot 21
    Don't Look Away – Immediately Anyway . . 21
    Put on Your Bedroom Eyes 22
    Gaze a Little Longer 23
    Look Him Over 24
    What About Him? 25
    Making It Work For You 25
    Wrapping Up 27

CHAPTER 4: Let's Pick Him Up! 29
    How it Works 31
    Wrapping Up 32

Chapter 5: And Let's Not Forget Body Language . 33
Dance Step 1: The Non-Verbal Signal 33
Dance Step 2: Verbal Signal 33
Dance Step 3: Turn 34
Dance Step 4: The Fleeting Touch 34
Dance Step 5: Synchronize Your Watches… . 35
The Steps 36
Forget Your Upbringing 37
Remember, Soften 38
Wrapping Up 41

Chapter 6: It's Finally Time to Focus on Your Conversation! 43
Have Opinions 43
Watch His Body Language 44
But Gregg…I Just Met Him!
How do I Know What to Talk About? 46
Wrapping Up 49

Chapter 7: Talking Like You're Already in Love . . 51
Level 1: Social 51
Level 2: Facts 52
Level 3: Personal 52
Level 4: "We" 53
Great, Now What? 53
Share Carefully 54
A Note on Listening 55
Wrapping Up 56

Chapter 8: Sharing Your Story 57
Always Be Prepared 57
Know Your Audience 59
A Note on Confidence 60
Wrapping Up 61

Chapter 9: He Needs to EARN a Date 63
What Does It Mean to Get Busy? 63
Write Your Story 65
Wrapping Up. 67

Chapter 10: The Best First Date 69
Heighten The Emotion 69
We're Really The Same. 71
When Dining Out 73
Let Him Be A Guy 73
What To Wear 74
Wrapping Up. 75

Chapter 11: We're so (Un)Alike 77
Sort Of Similar. 78
Talk Alike 80
Being Class Conscious. 81
Wrapping Up. 83

Chapter 12: Three Crucial Ways to Be Similar .. 85
Similar Interests 85
Similar Beliefs 87
Similar Attitudes About Love & Relationships 89
But How? 92
This Seems Like A Lot of Work 92
Wrapping Up. 93

Chapter 13: You...Complete Me 95
How Do You Unearth What's Important To Him? 96
Accentuate The Positive 96
Wrapping Up. 98

Chapter 14: Don't Make a Man Your Hobby ... 99
What IS Making A Man Your Hobby?. ... 99
How To Avoid Making Him Your Hobby .. 100
Other Benefits Of Hobbies. 101
Wrapping Up. 103

Chapter 15: Support Who He Thinks He Is ... 105
Step 1: He's Captivating. 106
Step 2: Show Empathy 106
Step 3: The Implied Compliment 107
Step 4: The Compliment 107
Step 5: The Killer Compliment 114
Who Needs A Compliment 115
Laugh At (All of) His Jokes 116
Have Pet Names 116
Receiving His Praise & Compliments 117
Wrapping Up. 117

Chapter 16: Keep The Home Fires Burning ... 119
Intimacy Isn't Sex 119
How To Build Intimacy. 120
Learn His Love Language. 123
Wrapping Up. 125

Conclusions 127

Author Bio. 131

Get the Word Out to Your Friends 136

Introduction

CAN YOU REALLY MAKE SOMEONE FALL IN LOVE WITH YOU?

No doubt you're already shaking your head, wondering if I've completely gone off the deep end. A book on how to make a man fall in love with me, Gregg?? Really? Come on…

Yes.

Well, okay sort of. There are both overt and covert tactics on how to make a man fall in love with you.

I call them *Night Moves!*

This book isn't about how to *force* someone to fall in love with you and I don't plan to teach you that. What I'm here for is to give you every advantage in helping the process along and very few women know it.

Now, back to the original question. Can you really make someone fall in love with you? Yes and no. What we're going to do is look at the science behind why people fall in love and then use that to your advantage to make it happen.

What???

I know. Stay with me.

The truth is that there are a lot of things happening in your body when you first see someone new – things you are completely unaware of. For example, when a woman spots an attractive man for the first time, her pupils dilate. Who knew, right? Now, let's be clear, I am not a proponent of love at first sight, not at all. In fact, quite the opposite, however, I do believe you can draw someone in or push them away more easily than you think. The facts don't lie, so why not give yourself every advantage you can, including science!?

GREGG, WHAT *ABOUT* LOVE AT FIRST SIGHT?

Love at first sight is really love at first *hind*sight. Let's imagine for a moment you're in the supermarket. Across the tomato display, you spot him – a true Adonis. You're nearly speechless. Your heart is all fluttery, your knees feel wobbly and oh my, am I perspiring all of a sudden!?! All physical responses to, not love, but attraction. This, my friend, is lust. Now, let's suppose your Adonis walks by and crashes into you, knocking your tomatoes onto the ground, busting them up and making a huge mess. He doesn't even stop to say as much as "Uh sorry". How's he lookin' now? You're probably ready to deck him and all of a sudden, you're not feeling anything but anger.

Suppose, on the other hand, that same Adonis walked up with a thick Jamaican (insert your favorite accent here) accent. He suavely says something like, "Excuse me Ma'am but I think you dropped this" as he hands you the produce bag you dropped, along with your jaw, when you first saw him. He smiles a crooked little smile at you and you're sunk.

In the first instance, you felt lust that went into "what a jerk" mode. In the second example, you may indeed go out with this guy and fall in love with him. In either case, your first response – all of the sweating and beating heart stuff – that was lust.

OKAY SO HOW THEN?

Right! You're anxious to find out how to make Adonis fall in love with you. I get it. That's what the rest of the book is about! We're going to examine how men react to different stimuli and how to prepare yourself, when you go out, to meet Mr. Right. I know women who've met their husbands while pumping gas, at the grocery store, at the gym and at charity events. Mr. Right could be anywhere and the rest of this book is about how to prepare yourself, before you leave your house, to meet him, and what to do once he's in your sights.

Are you ready to get started?

Special Offer!

Find your knight in shining armor online quickly by getting my **free** report, *80 Ways to Read a Man*! In this custom report you will learn how to read the body language of a man! This report takes you through the male body, one area at a time and helps you decipher each move he makes. You'll know whether he's a nice guy with good intentions or a player trying to get into your pants.

www.whoholdsthecardsnow.com/sign-80-ways-read-man/

Chapter 1

WE'RE ALL JUST A BUNCH OF SOYBEANS

What would you say if I told you that we look at one another like we're commodities being traded on the open market?

Yes, you and I are soybeans. Let me explain.

When we look at a potential suitor we say, "What's in it for me?" We do. We might not think it out loud or even know it but we all think in those terms.

Who does Hollywood date? The plumber they use? The guy who fixes the stage lighting? Chances are they don't date those folks. Not because these are bad or inferior people, but because they are not in the same stratosphere as the actors or actresses. Would the plumber or the stage lighting person be happy with dating a Hollywood actor or actress? I doubt it, he or she would probably be happier with someone they have more in common with.

Is this fair? Maybe not, but it *is* reality. We tend to date people who have the same *equity* as the equity we perceive we have ourselves. We aren't looking for an exact match but we naturally tend to come pretty close.

If you rank in appearance as a 5 and you want to date a 10, good luck. This is one of the ways in which we make wrong selections for potential partners. I can contact every single woman on Rodeo Drive and I will get shot down. Why? Because I don't bring what they desire to the table. I don't bring their money, their looks, and the social class they are accustomed too.

It doesn't make them better than me and I don't take it personally. In fact, I know if Shakira did date me, it wouldn't last. Neither of us would be happy. Well, I might be for few weeks.

Science tells us that people are most happy when both parties get something equal out of the relationship. It's called the equity principle. Each party wants the best deal they can get so they look at a person's *market value*. The good news is everybody has a different perceived value. What might be an incredible man, or value, to you won't be to another woman.

Studies show that the more positive characteristics you bring to the table, the better success you will have finding love. Combine this with your mate having equal assets and your odds of finding your lifetime love partner explode!

This means that you are about equal in these 6 areas:

1. Looks
2. Amount of money you make
3. Intelligence
4. Status
5. Personality
6. Inner Nature

But Gregg, I see a beautiful woman dating an average man all the time.

That's because they balance out in some way. She might be better looking but he makes more money. They balance when you assess their relationship across all 6 categories. Another example might be an attractive man taking care of his wife who has a debilitating disease. They are not equal one might say, but in truth she took care of him when he was sick with cancer 10 years earlier so, again, things even out.

Why does the equity principle make sense? Because in a non-equal relationship, the partner bringing more assets to the table begins to feel deprived of something he or she feels they deserve. They may feel as if they're giving more than they're receiving out of the relationship. The unbalance grows and contempt begins to build.

The other partner often feels they are not worthy of someone with so much to offer, making them worry and lose their confidence. A man might feel emasculated. A woman might feel that she has nothing to offer him.

There was a girl in my high school who was gorgeous. My buddies and I couldn't get near her. She wasn't even that bright. We'll call her Beth. She went on to marry a gorgeous rich guy. She got pregnant and never lost the weight. Her husband started treating her like crap and they got divorced. Why? Because what she brought to the table was gone and he felt ripped off.

Fair? No. But it's the hard truth.

Your goal is to keep your equity as high as you can so you can date the best guy you can. My joke is, don't call me if you are 30K in debt, 30 pounds overweight, and driving a '98 Honda leaking oil. It's a joke but there is truth in it too. I want someone better, as selfish as that may sound and, I bet you do too.

Shakira is saying the same thing about me. "Gregg, don't call me at 5 foot 9, with your money and your terrible singing voice!"

If only she knew how good my shower voice was!

WRAPPING UP

Realize where you are in life and look to date an equal. You will be happier and your relationship more successful. Don't go for that 6 foot 5 stud driving the Ferrari unless you are a runway model who has a contract with Vogue. You won't be happy even if you can land him. Be realistic. Take care of the things that you can control.

Do this:

- Create a great story so you are as interesting as you can be
- Strive for the best career you can, but one you're passionate about
- Develop a high degree of self-esteem
- Understand men so you are not blind to how we think
- Take care of your body!
- Look great when you go out
- Get happy inside!
- Find one passion and become a pro at it

These are things you can control and they will make you into the best soybean you can be!

Chapter 2
YOU NEVER GET A SECOND CHANCE TO MAKE A FIRST IMPRESSION

I know, it's cliché. Let me have this one, okay? The truth of falling in love with someone is that the first impression is something many never forget. You'll hear elderly couples telling you what the other wore the first time they met, maybe more than 60 years earlier. It matters. Is it possible to meet Adonis when you're running around in your grubby sweats, leaves in your hair and no makeup? It can happen, sure, but the more likely time Adonis is going to notice you is when you're wearing lipstick.

Huh?

We'll circle back to that in a minute. The truth is that there are things men notice about women when they first see them. If you know me at all, you know I make no apologies for my gender. Men are animals. I can't state it any differently. We're animals. Ultimately, when we choose a woman, we *do* go for things like values and all of that other stuff, but when it comes to first impressions… well it is what it is.

In my book, *To Date a Man, You Must Understand a Man*, I spend a lot of time trying to help you understand how the male mind operates. Women often give us too much credit for thinking things through, often because you *do* think things through and expect we are the same. This leads to frustration on your end. Anyway, men and women don't do many things in the same way when it comes to relationships. That's probably why the divorce rate is high and why around 50% of all Americans are single. The sooner you come to accept this first truth, the easier your dating and relationship life will become.

MEN ARE VISUAL

Don't shoot the messenger, but men are visual. We are constantly looking around a room for the attractive woman. This is evolutionary as it turns out. The caveman, who spent the most time looking about the seaside for the most attractive, most 'able to carry his babies' woman, survived while the ones who banged the first cavewoman they saw eventually died off. I know, you think some of them still hang around…those men today are called players.

This is evolutionary because when the caveman found the cavewoman attractive, he was more inclined to want to mate with her, thus sending his genetic code a little further down the line. He chose a woman with broader hips and one who seemed more likely to successfully conceive. Meanwhile, the lesser caveman banged every woman he saw but somehow managed not to impregnate any of them.

What this means to you is men are always looking but that doesn't mean they want to buy. So many women get jealous over the wandering eye of their man. Stop it. He's just window shopping. Much like you're just looking at those $500 pumps in the shoe store window, he's just looking. It also means that the odds of a man looking your way any time you're out and about are pretty good, yet you're probably oblivious to most of them.

Therefore, in order to be seen, you need to make yourself *available*. Let me explain. What I mean by this is don't sit in the back row of a book club you've joined, you know –to meet new people. Don't hide behind the wall divider at social events, hoping to go unnoticed. Adonis won't find you there. Put yourself in view of other men. Don't use your sunglasses or hat as a smokescreen either. We want to see your beautiful eyes. Let me see you. That's your first lesson!

ACTIVITY #1: BE SEEN

This is an especially important activity for you if you're on the shy side. I'm not telling you to dance an Irish jig the next time you go get coffee, but instead of driving through, go inside and get your coffee. Sit down at one of the tables and relax for a few moments. Don't hide behind a newspaper either – that's cheating! If you want a distraction, drag your laptop with you but don't seem unapproachable. Look up and around the room from time to time. If you see someone attractive, lock gazes with him for a few seconds (more on this later).

WHAT IS ATTRACTIVE?

Good news. No two men define attractive in the same way. Yes, some men want the tall blonde with the deep blue eyes, but some men prefer a woman who is a little heavier or one with short brunette hair. For some men, it's the smile or legs. Every man is different in what he feels is attractive. This is good news to every woman because, as luck would have it, you're all different!

So, yes, men are looking for *attractive* women, but each man's definition of attractive is different. It's like in the movie, *White Christmas*, when the two fellas go to listen to the two sisters sing for the first time. One makes mention of "her blue eyes" while the other is ogling over "her brown eyes", then they realize they're both looking at a different sister, finding them both attractive.

There are studies which indicate that our definition of attractiveness has roots in our childhood. If a man had a close relationship with his mother and she wore a certain perfume, he will be drawn to that perfume. If she wore her hair a certain way, he might be attracted to a woman with a similar hairstyle. Word has it that Conrad Hilton found his wife by her red hat, which he saw a few rows ahead of him in church one Sunday. He followed that red hat until he met the woman beneath it and eventually married her. Probably because someone he loved in his childhood wore a red hat.

Don't blast me for this section. I know the beauty of individuals is more than skin deep, but that's what dating is for. We're talking about attraction right here and you can't dig that deep staring across the tomatoes at Adonis.

ACTIVITY #2: AN ATTRACTIVENESS AFFIRMATION

Many women don't believe they're attractive enough to meet a man. I know a woman who wouldn't post her photograph on online dating sites because the first man she met offline commented on her weight. She lost all confidence in her attractiveness based on one idiot. She resigned herself to being single. Your job is to begin believing you're attractive, so here's what I want you to do. First, listen to what you say to yourself now about your attractiveness. Once you've done that for a couple of days, I want you to turn it around and begin telling yourself you *are* attractive. Over and over, hear those words "I am an attractive woman". Say it as many times as you can until you believe it.

WHAT ELSE DO MEN "LOOK" AT?

When it comes to first glances, a lot happens in a short amount of time. Let's imagine Adonis is still in the produce aisle. He's spotted you and he's spotted another female. You've got that down-home, earthy look going on. Relaxed but classy. The other woman is wearing spike heels, has her hair pulled up tight into a bun and is wearing really expensive-looking business attire. He may choose you over her if he feels intimidated by the more powerful looking woman. It may make him feel as if he would be sexually inadequate with her.

Now, on the other hand, if Adonis is into the high power woman, she may win out in the game you don't even know you're playing. Again, it's all in what he finds attractive. Men are always screening, maybe not even consciously. "Will she be able to carry my children?" This could translate into things like her body shape – something he may not even realize he's considering.

Facial beauty, again in the eye of the beholder, is often associated with grace, intelligence and popularity. If he finds your face attractive, he will associate those qualities with you before he knows who you are inside.

ACTIVITY #3: FIND YOU

When you go on dates, you should be comfortable. I know women get all wrapped up in wearing just the right outfits and accessorizing with just the right pieces, but the truth is that most (straight) men wouldn't know a Coach purse if it hit them upside the head and the ones who do know that brand will find you to be high maintenance. Rather than try to impress him with an expensive look which really doesn't represent who you are, relax and be yourself.

Look in your closet and identify some first date outfits you can wear which really speak to who you are. What's comfortable? What says "Here comes Julia, take her or leave her"? That's what you want to wear. If it's a tie-died wrap skirt from the 70's, so be it. That's who you are. Learn to live in your own skin and be who you are!

HOW DO YOU KNOW?

I often tell women to go for the silent guy – the one who is awkwardly trying to talk to them. Root for this guy. This guy is most likely tongue-tied because he's so smitten with you. He has looked you over and you fit his idea of the ideal woman. Your facial features feel comfortable and familiar to him, you have the eyes, chest, butt or legs he's into (usually just one of those) and you may have even mentioned something in passing in which he's interested, "Yeah I volunteer at the local shelter twice a month helping vaccinate cats." Well, since I love cats, you can guess I'm now even more intrigued!

A man who seems disinterested in you may either be truly disinterested or he may feel intimidated by you. This isn't your fault. Don't let men tell you otherwise. It's their own insecurity getting in the way. Many men can't handle being in a relationship with a woman who makes more money than they do or has a more powerful position. Some men rule out certain professions as being too intimidating – doctors and lawyers (I'm afraid of lawyers) for example. Another man may find this same woman fascinating and not be intimidated by her at all.

A man who is interested might go unnoticed by you, so you need to be paying some attention. A lot will depend on your attitude going in. Are you going into the situation ready to meet a man or are you feeling jilted and bitter toward men? Men can sniff out bitterness about as easily as they can sniff out beer and pizza before a football game. Before you can be successful, you're going to need to get rid of that jilted and bitter feeling.

You know he's interested when you catch him looking at you. You know if he seems to be tongue-tied and awkward. You know if he walks past and maybe brushes against you or finds a reason to make a passing comment like, "Boy I sure hope the Pats make it to the Super Bowl again this year" or something equally innocuous. The problem many of us have is admitting to ourselves that someone else could actually be interested. We don't believe in our own attractiveness so we don't look for the cues that someone else might be interested. Remember, he fears rejection too, especially if he's a little shy.

WHAT'S A GIRL TO DO?

Okay here are a few things research has shown will help you attract a man's attention:

- Wear red – it makes you appear warmer and more confident
- Laugh at his jokes – yes it's an ego stroke but give a guy a break, okay?

- Be honest – there is no point pretending you like dogs if you don't, the truth always comes out
- Mirror his actions – this shows interest and attraction
- Go out with other women – men find women more attractive when they're in a group
- Develop positive personality traits like kindness, assertiveness and openness
- If you own a dog, take Fido out for a walk – people with dogs are almost 90% more approachable and dog ownership has been found to make you more attractive
- Spare the makeup – men don't find piled on make-up attractive but prefer a natural look
- When you do put on the makeup, don't forget the lipstick – men find lipstick very appealing, especially red or pink
- Be the girl next door – men prefer curvy women with size 14's beating out the size 8's of the world; don't beat yourself up if you're not bone thin

WRAPPING UP

- Let your hair down, literally; your odds of being less intimidating are much greater if you relax your look

- Learn to appreciate your strengths and stop being your own worst critic

- Leave the office at the office at the end of the day; go into an evening out with the girls as one of the girls, not boss-lady

- Pay attention to your surroundings and take note of men who might be sizing you up; more tips on how to entice him are coming soon!

- Don't be a wall flower; put yourself 'out there' and get noticed!

- When you leave the house, leave knowing you might run into Adonis – be mentally and physically prepared (i.e. don't wear the grubby sweats and get the leaves out of your hair!)

Chapter 3

FIRING THE FIRST SHOT

Your job, as the female half of the relationship equation, is to create the spark, ideally without him even knowing it's happened. Let's examine a few ways in which you can make this happen.

DON'T LOOK AWAY – IMMEDIATELY ANYWAY

When we lock eyes with someone, it triggers a very primitive part of the brain to react. That part of the brain tells you to do one of two things – approach or retreat. When you maintain eye contact with someone for several seconds, it stirs in them a reaction similar to fear. Phenyl ethylamine or PEA is released, inducing the feeling of love.

For this reason, one thing you want to do is make strong, intense eye contact with Adonis. Let's look at the basics of this. Let's say you're on a trip to Paris. You're riding along in a cab, fearing for your life as you zip through traffic when, suddenly, you look out the window and there it is – the Eiffel Tower. All of a sudden you can't stop looking at it. You're so taken by the awesome thing you're looking at, that you don't want to look away. The same holds true for humans. We associate looking at someone or something for a long period of time as showing our interest in that person or thing. When we are bored with something, the first thing to remove itself from the scene is our eyes.

How often have you been in a meeting where someone is droning on and on about nothing. Look around the room at how many people seemingly just got bombarded with "must read" emails on their phones. They averted their eyes from the speaker because he was no longer interesting or appealing.

If you find yourself in a conversation with Adonis, you want to maintain eye contact for roughly 75% of the time you're together. This is probably enough time for him to begin feeling attracted to you. The trick is you must look directly into his eyes, not at his eyebrows, not at his chin or forehead, but his eyes. If you've seen *Monster-In-Law*, you've seen the part where the handsome young doctor is so smitten with the dog walker/artist/receptionist. She feels he's full of crap so she quickly turns away and says "What's the color of my eyes". He, of course, pulls out some long dreamy description of the color of her eyes, immediately telling her he's for real. Okay so it's a movie but it still works!

PUT ON YOUR BEDROOM EYES

What are bedroom eyes? Simply put, dilated pupils. It seems, through research, scientists have discovered that it is the eye to eye gazing that gets folks *in the mood*, not looking at each other naked or watching porn first.

It's the eye-to-eye contact that really gets the old motor purring.

But how can you make your own pupils dilate? When you're talking to a man, there is invariably some part of him you find attractive. Studies have shown that when you fix your gaze on that part of his anatomy you find attractive, your pupils will grow. Just avoid something about him you don't find attractive or they'll slam shut again!

Along with looking at his wonderful features, think about how attractive he is to you. Do a little dreaming about the two of you in the sack. It is crucial that you do this with confidence. If you're shy, nervous, apprehensive or mistrustful, your pupils won't dilate and you won't be able to woo him in with those bedroom eyes.

One more note on bedroom eyes – studies have shown that when a man looks at a woman whose pupils are dilated, his pupils dilate to match. That's a win my friend, that's a win.

GAZE A LITTLE LONGER

Research also tell us that couples who are in love will continue looking into one another's eyes through a silence or break in their conversation. The bond and attraction are so strong between them that they can't take their eyes off one another. Therefore, when you're talking with Adonis and the conversation breaks, keep looking in his eyes for a few seconds. You're still stirring that primal thing inside him and you're simulating love. If you do pull your eyes away, do it slowly and dreamily, as if you're reluctant to do so.

LOOK HIM OVER

While he's talking, take your eyes off of his eyes and begin looking at his other features. Slowly move to his hair, maybe his cheekbones or the cute dimple on his chin. He will notice. Don't be creepy about it but just slowly travel your eyes over first his face, then move down to his neck and shoulders. You're still stirring the same primal instincts in him.

Beware, though, if this seems to make him super uncomfortable, stop it and go back to his eyes. We don't want to scare him off. Return your gaze, from time to time, to his eyes and hold your contact there again.

This eye contact is such a big deal. We do it without realizing many times. If you've attended a seminar or a show where there is a person up on a stage talking, you will often see them fix eyes on someone in the audience. It's probably someone who has their gaze fixed on the speaker. This is because the person in the audience finds the speaker interesting. You're showing genuine interest in a man when you fix your eyes on his. It's a subliminal way of saying, "I find you interesting".

WHAT ABOUT HIM?

One way to tell if a man is looking at you with potential for love is to follow *his* eyes. If he's looking at your eyes, or even your face, he's more inclined to feel love for you than lust. If, however, his eyes wander to different parts of your body and stay there, he's most likely just feeling lustful. He doesn't realize he's doing this, mind you, so don't get angry. It's just your way of knowing how *he* is feeling toward you at that moment.

Having said all of that, you should understand that his first, brief glances may be at your body. He's literally sizing you up, but not in an offensive way. As I mentioned previously, some men are leg men, some are butt guys and still others go for the chest. Odds are, he'll at least spend a couple seconds looking in those areas first but, your test comes when he looks into your eyes and doesn't stop.

MAKING IT WORK FOR YOU

So how do you make this work for you? There are a few things you can do to help this process along. Let's examine these.

DON'T FOCUS ON "THE PROCESS"

If you're a highly anxious person, you might psych yourself out so remember to relax and focus on just his eyes. Don't worry about exactly following some set of steps. All you need to know is that if you want him to feel as if he's falling in love with you, you need to gaze into his eyes. Remember to look at or think about something you enjoy so you dilate those pupils, thus enhancing the effect.

LET THE GAZE GO SLOWLY

Remember to take your eyes away slowly, as if they're being dragged away. It's painful to take your eyes off of someone who intrigues you so much.

By the same token, though, don't come off as creepy. There's a fine line between gazing into someone's eyes and staring at them. If you're looking directly into his eyes and you are feeling an emotional connection, it shouldn't feel creepy. If he seems, however, to be creeped out by your gaze, avert your eyes for about a minute and look back.

Remember, you've caused his fight or flight chemicals to kick in so he's feeling initially a little bit of a chemical rush and he doesn't know quite what to do with it.

Staring is when you are looking at someone as if to size them up or question in your mind what on earth possessed them to pick out that outfit today. Staring is rude and people are rightly put off by it. If you were raised not to stare, it's important for you to make this distinction.

ACTIVITY #4: PRACTICE, PRACTICE, PRACTICE!

If you're truly uncomfortable staring into someone's eyes, get a friend with whom you're comfortable and ask them to allow you to gaze into their eyes. They can do the same back. The more you practice, the less "forced" it will feel for you, and for them. Just try not to turn it into a giggle fest!

WRAPPING UP

- If you want a man to feel as if he's in love with you, gaze into his eyes
- The size of your pupils determines how he responds – if your pupils are wide open, he's going to feel that from you and likely reciprocate
- To enlarge pupils, look at the part of him you find most attractive or think about the two of you in a very enjoyable activity
- Don't force it – if you feel that's what is happening, stop, you're probably not really feeling it and neither is he
- Practice! Get a good friend to practice this with you – it will help you train your pupils to respond

Chapter 4
LET'S PICK HIM UP!

No, I'm not going to teach you to be some sleazy pick up artist who runs around snagging men with her big-pupil gaze and wandering eyes. I am going to teach you how to continue this process of making a man fall in love with you. While many think the world of picking up someone is mostly male, research tells us that more than 2/3 of women have made the first move. Times they are a'changin'!

Researcher Monica Moore, upon hearing this statistic, set out to observe women picking up men. In her study, she took note of how many times women performed different actions which resulted in a man approaching. Her observations of more than 200 women in social settings determined the following:

- Women smiled broadly at a man successfully 511 times
- Short, darting glances were successfully thrown in the direction of a man 253 times

- 253 women danced alone and caught the attention of a man
- One hundred and thirty-nine times, a woman looked straight at a man and flipped her hair, resulting in a visit from said man
- There were 117 instances where a woman kept a fixed gaze on a man and he approached.

Those are your top sellers. Things which worked but less frequently in this study included:

- Looking at a man, tossing your head and looking back at him
- Accidentally brushing up against a man
- Nodding your head at a man
- Pointing at the chair next to you and inviting a man to sit
- Tilting your head and touching your exposed neck
- Licking your lips during eye contact
- Primping while keeping eye contact with him
- Parading close to a man with exaggerated hip movement
- Asking for help with something
- Tapping something to get his attention
- Patting his behind (although not advisable)

If you feel this is too forward, or if your mother "raised you better than that", think of it this way – it's your evolutionary duty to lure him in. You're just facilitating the procreation process. If you're past that phase of life, as many single women today are, forget the procreation and just consider it going after what you want!

If you're still bothered by this, let me confess something to you which should help. Even though you may make one of these gestures or movements in the direction of a man, his ego will kick in pretty quickly and he won't remember the story that way a few minutes later. He will firmly believe *he* picked *you* up.

Have some fun with this – its science!

ACTIVITY #5: SMILE

I want you to focus on smiling at a few men. When you're pumping gas or at the supermarket, wherever you are, smile. It may take a few smiles to actually entice a man to approach anyway so trying it once will be good practice.

HOW IT WORKS

The pickup activities above might not work if just tried once. In fact, you'll most likely need to make eye contact with a man a few times before he approaches. This is normal and you shouldn't give up just because it didn't work on the first try. If you're really set on meeting this guy, try a few times over several minutes. Keep an eye on him. When he looks in your direction, flash him your pearly whites. He'll probably nervously look away. That's okay. Wait for it….waaaaaaaaaaaaait for it. He'll look in your direction again and what do you do? Yup! You flash him that smile again. He may again look nervously away but chances are he'll step up his efforts this time, maybe subconsciously.

He may now walk by you, you know – to go to the bathroom or to get another drink – and he may even brush up against you. Smile again. When he walks by the other way, you guessed it – smile. Eventually, he will indeed find himself breaking the ice with you and trust me when I say he will believe it was all *his idea* all along. Don't burst his bubble – let him have this one.

WRAPPING UP

- Remember not to focus too much on "the process", relax and enjoy the hunt
- If all else fails, keep smiling at him when you notice he's looking in your direction
- Rest assured that a man won't find you too forward – even a few minutes after you start talking to him, his ego will kick in and he'll believe he picked you up

Chapter 5

AND LET'S NOT FORGET BODY LANGUAGE

Dr. Timothy Perper, determined to uncover the body language of attraction, perched himself on a barstool for more than 2,000 hours, observing the actions of men and women.[1] From this perch high atop the bar scene, Dr. Perper developed what he called *The Dance of Intimacy*. Perper discovered that when people performed these steps in the proper order, they left as a couple or with plans to date soon. When even one step was missed, it was game over. What are the steps Dr. Perper uncovered?

DANCE STEP 1: THE NON-VERBAL SIGNAL
We just talked about this in the last chapter. This is your dancing alone or your gaze into his eyes. It's something you do subtly to send a signal to his PEA that you're interested. The unsuspecting male's chemical process has now been ignited and it's your job to continue fanning the flames.

DANCE STEP 2: VERBAL SIGNAL
This is where you talk. This doesn't mean a full-blown conversation. It could be something as simple as "Hello"

---

1. Dr. Timothy Perper, *Sex Signals: The Biology of Love*, Isi Pr, 1985.

or "Hi". If there's a game on the TV where you are, you might say something like "How about those Indians this season?" or "Too bad about that Steelers loss last week". You could also ask a question like "is that an Apple watch? I was thinking about getting one of those!" Whatever you say, this signal opens the door a little further.

DANCE STEP 3: TURN

Once you speak, or he speaks to you, the person being spoken to must turn to face the speaker. Just the head is likely to turn, but this acknowledgement must occur. Once the person turns to face the speaker, conversation will follow.

From here, further turning will begin. It's like watching wind chimes slowly turn in the wind – first the shoulders will turn in the direction of the speaker, then the full torso, then the knees and finally, maybe not at the first meeting but definitely in subsequent meetings, they will be full body to full body facing one another. Pretty cool, eh? The important thing is that the initial head turn occurs.

One note on this turning sequence – it could take just a few minutes or it could take hours. There is no set time limit on this sequence occurring. Just be patient and observe.

DANCE STEP 4: THE FLEETING TOUCH

Delivering a subtle touch might go unnoticed but it's still observable and important. This can come in the form of plucking a piece of lint off of a sweater or brushing against someone's hand when they reach for a nacho or pretzel. It's casual and brief but important. How you react is crucial.

Let's say Adonis walks up to you in the tomato aisle after you've thrown your best gaze in his direction. He may say, "Let me help you with that" and then you respond with something like, "Thanks". You and Adonis are now conversing. Maybe you talk about how the tomatoes are never as ripe looking in the winter or something like that. Then it happens. Adonis reaches for his own produce bag and brushes his hand across yours as he does so.

If you're into Adonis, you'll probably react warmly but if you tense up or pull your hand away, Adonis will view this as rejection and he'll likely pick up his tomatoes and shop on without you. If you respond warmly, you will likely see the eye contact change. It will be less *forced* and more interested in nature. He may begin to study your face and body, looking you over again, more seriously this time.

DANCE STEP 5: SYNCHRONIZE YOUR WATCHES...

Alright, not your watches but just about everything else will begin to synchronize. You both reach for your drinks at the same time and replace them at the same time. You turn in unison to a disturbance or to the music change. You begin to mirror one another's actions. Once the movement is over, eyes will return to one another as if nothing happened.

Synchronicity will often last until nature kicks in and one or both parties leaves the venue. By this time, however, they may be making plans to see one another again. At the very least, they've exchanged phone numbers.

THE STEPS

Dr. Perper's study indicated that if any step along the way was missed, the potential for the two to become a couple was sidetracked. Even if you get all the way to step 5 but don't have synchronicity, it's game over.

The good news is that you can make this happen. These are all deliberate actions you can take to keep the interaction moving forward. We've talked a lot about the first step – the non-verbal step. Step 2 might be difficult for you if you're shy but it's one you can't skip so it's time to figure it out. Step 3 is only up to you if you are the one being spoken to. If you speak to a man and he doesn't turn in your direction, you may need to start over with the non-verbal cues on someone else. Odds are he's just not that into you.

If you do make conversation, you can certainly be the one to initiate Steps 4 and 5 – brushing up against him and moving in synchronization with him.

This would be a great time to read my best seller, *The Social Tigress*, so you can get even more tactics to attract a man at a social venue. I will give it to you for **FREE!** Email me at Gregg@WhoHoldsTheCardsNow.com and mention the word, "TIGRESS" And if you would be so kind to leave me a review on this book or any of my books, I would greatly appreciate it!

ACTIVITY #6: WHAT MAKES YOU UNCOMFORTABLE?

Chances are, one or more of the "Dance Steps" above makes you a tad uncomfortable. Those are the steps you need to work on, independent of trying to meet a man. We already talked about practicing looking into someone's eyes. Practice just saying "Hi" to a passing stranger if the thought of talking to a stranger scares you. Make sure you practice all elements of the step, like turning toward someone who speaks to you.

FORGET YOUR UPBRINGING

Depending on how old you are, you may or may not have been brought up to be a strong, independent woman. Great. I'm all for it but, the problem is that this doesn't do a thing for the male ego. **Men love the chase.** If you don't allow him to chase you, he won't be excited by the relationship and he *needs* to be excited.

What this means to you is that you need to toss your feminism aside for certain aspects of dating. This can be confusing so stay with me. There are aspects of your strong side I want you to keep and things I want you to set aside. Let's first look at what you need to set aside.

In order for him to feel as if he's chasing, you need to avoid pushing yourself on him. Let him ask for the first date, or the second. Let him text you following that date to tell you he had a great time. Let him set up some of your dates, especially early on. He's chasing you and he's trying really hard right now to hold your interest. Let him. Yes, it's okay for you to plan a date but let him do it first. Yes, it's okay to text him and say what a great time you had but don't expect a lengthy conversation and let him do it for the first date.

What you can keep is your offer to pay your half of the date. If you're going bowling, offer to pay your own shoe rental and part of the fees. If you're going to dinner, offer to pay for your own meal or drinks. If he offers to pay for the whole thing, you can say something like, "Okay but the next one's on me, okay?" This is important because it tells him you aren't in it for his money. By offering to pay your half, you're offering to keep things on an even playing field. Don't offer to buy the whole meal, especially the first time you go out, just your half.

REMEMBER, SOFTEN

I know you're going to panic. You'll find yourself staring at Adonis, maybe not over the tomatoes but maybe at a social gathering and you're going to freak out. Worst of all, you won't have this book to go back to so I'm going to give you a tool you can remember. Soften.

What?

S means you smile at him. Remember, more than 500 women got a man to approach her just by smiling at him with a broad smile. Don't forget to make eye contact when you do so! It may take a few smiles to get him to approach!

O reminds you to have open body language. We didn't really talk about this but let's briefly go over it now. Open body language means your eyes are forward, not looking down. Your arms aren't crossed in front of you. You have a look about you that says, "Sure, handsome, you can come talk to me" so some poor schmuck won't pee himself trying it. This is another opportunity to gaze into his eyes, even if only for a second or two.

F tells you to lean forward. This body language is important. It shows you're interested in the person you're talking to or about to talk to. You don't have to bend at the waist or anything dramatic, just sort of lean in. You certainly don't want him to think you're trying to kiss him, just be subtle enough to show interest.

T says touch him, as we discussed. Just a brief brush of his arm or across his hand as you pick something up or reach for something. Again, this is subtle. You're not trying to knock his drink out of his hand, just barely graze as you go by.

E is where your eyes come into play. You've already gotten his attention a few times by looking at him and looking away. Now that you're one-on-one, it's time to really use eye contact to your advantage. Gaze into his baby blues or browns and slowly turn your eyes away. As you get to know one another, this shouldn't require any effort. It will naturally happen.

N means you nod as he speaks. Not all of the time, but nod to show you're paying attention and you're in agreement with what he's saying, even if you're not. This isn't the time to debate which candidate you're voting for or whether or not women should get equal pay, it's the time for casual conversation where you can get to know one another. Your nod is a subconscious acknowledgement to him – an ego stroke.

ACTIVITY #7: BODY LANGUAGE

Your body language comes into play in this chapter and in chapters to follow. It's time to start taking note of your body language and the body language of others. Does someone have their arms crossed? This signals closed body language – someone who is unapproachable. Do you do this? Nod when someone speaks to you. Lean in when someone is talking to you. Practicing better body language for yourself and beginning to observe that of others will help you be more comfortable doing it later.

WRAPPING UP

- You can covertly use body language to get a man's attention; a first, non-verbal signal will tell a guy you're interested in him

- A small word or two, maybe a question or statement made to a man can help break the ice, especially if he's a little shy; don't be afraid to say something as you walk by

- Learn your 5 steps: non-verbal, verbal, turn, touch and synchronize; it's like a dance step you need to learn

- By all means, SOFTEN (most of which is covered in your 5 steps)

Chapter 6

IT'S FINALLY TIME TO FOCUS ON YOUR CONVERSATION!

I don't think there is anything more nerve-wracking than a first conversation between two people on a first date. It's awkward and scary, to say the least. The problem is this is an important conversation and you can't just get your phone out and start checking today's news. While you're not actually going on that first date yet, it's time to think about preparing for it.

HAVE OPINIONS

The most important thing you can do is to go into a first date well-rounded. Start paying enough attention to the world around you to at least have an opinion on things. I know you're sick of hearing about politics or football or whatever is hot news at that time but it might be an important topic to him so you need to at least know where the Bulls play versus the Bills (and what they play…hint, they're 2 different sports).

Once you're feeling a little more on top of current events, you should strive to have opinions about things. No man wants to hear "Ohhhh, I don't know…what do *you* think, Steve?" He wants to have friendly banter with you, much like he would with his buddies. So if he says something like, "I hope the Patriots make it to the Super Bowl this year again", you can come back with, "Yeah it doesn't look like those injuries are going to keep them down" or something appropriate. I'm not telling you to suddenly become a sports aficionado but have some opinions about a few topics. As you get to know him, you can fine tune what you know to fit the topics he's interested in. If you're lucky, he'll do the same, although I have to tell you it's scant few men who will be highly interested in the latest shoe styles or which color of purse goes with which dress. Save that stuff for your girlfriends!

If you need help in this area, I strongly recommend you read *To Date a Man You Must Understand Yourself*.

ACTIVITY #8: WHAT DO YOU CARE ABOUT?

Don't be Julia Roberts' character in *Runaway Bride*. Know what kind of eggs you like, what your political preferences are, whether or not you like football, baseball, surfing or hockey. What type of music do you like? Have something to talk about so when Adonis shows up at the grocery store, you're all set.

WATCH HIS BODY LANGUAGE

As you're chatting, you may find yourself talking about something you're interested in. Watch his body language. If he turns his head or body away, folds his arms around you or gets fidgety, he's lost interest. Ask him a question about himself to recover, "Oh geeze, listen to me. Where do you enjoy going to get good salmon?" or whatever. Engage him in a topic you know he's interested in.

Other signals of his interest or lack thereof would be if his face seems to 'fall' or brighten up and become livelier. You've struck a chord either way. Either change the subject or keep talking, depending. If you find something that lights him up, keep that conversation going for a while. If you express a shared interest or love in something he loves, at some point he will transfer his love of that thing to you. You might not know a lot about antique automobiles now, but if you make an effort to learn before you see him again, he'll be wowed!

Remember what we've talked about as far as eye contact goes? Well, if he breaks eye contact for a small reason and doesn't come back in pretty short order, you've lost him and it's time to bring it back home. Smoothly change the subject to re-engage his interest.

The same goes with his body. Not only does turning his eyes or head away show disinterest but so does turning his body away. The football game on television shouldn't be more interesting than his conversation with you, unless it's a national championship or something and even then, he shouldn't be focusing much on that if he's truly enamored with you. If he turns away physically or steps backward from you for more than a brief second, it's time to shift gears.

His hands can also tell you a lot! If someone begins fiddling with something or running a finger around the rim of their glass, they're contemplating something. This is a cue for you to slow down or be quiet for a moment so they can carefully consider what you're saying. If he talks and points his finger a lot, you can think of it sort of like a mini-erection. He feels very strongly about whatever he's saying and it's your cue to step in and be in full agreement.

Finally, don't forget his eyes. Much like your eyes, his tell a story. Your widened pupils attracted him, and if he was attracted to you, his widened as well. Now, it's time to keep an eye on his pupils. Narrowing pupils mean he's bored while wider pupils mean he's truly interested in what you're saying. Keep going on that topic.

BUT GREGG…I JUST MET HIM! HOW DO I KNOW WHAT TO TALK ABOUT?

I'm sure you don't think I'd leave you high and dry on this do you? Of course not! I've never left a damsel in distress! In order to figure out what he's interested in, all you need to do is pay attention.

Excuse me? Pay attention? That's IT?

That's it. He will drop hints about what he's interested in and if you're paying attention, you'll pick them up. Let's try one to see how well you do.

We have 2 main characters for our story, Adonis (of course) and Julia. Adonis is waiting in line at the coffee shop when Julia walks in, getting in line right behind him, and boy it's a long line. Adonis turns and says something like, "Boy I hope this line moves fast!" Julia, not wanting to be rude but also awestruck by his great looks and smooth accent says, "Me too! I'm going to be late if it doesn't."

Now, our hero, Adonis says, "Yeah. I was planning to stop by the animal shelter after work but if I don't get in on time, I might not have a chance."

Julia has a few choices here. Either she noticed the hint he just inadvertently dropped and she picks up the conversation there; she gets quiet because she doesn't know what else to say; or she says something else, completely missing his cue.

And what *was* his cue? "The shelter". This guy cares about animals. You don't know if he was stopping by to volunteer or to get a pet but what you do know is he likes animals. If you're an animal lover yourself, you two should have an instant spark. Even if you're not, you can show interest, "Oh wow, do you volunteer there or are you looking to adopt?" Now, you've got a conversation! He dropped that hint, really without knowing it, and gave you a perfect topic to keep the conversation going.

If Adonis doesn't say anything to clue you in, you need to engage him **and** find a subject he is interested in. What is he wearing? A sports cap? Know the team and ask about the Indians or whoever his sports allegiance is too. Is he wearing a t-shirt with some phrase or emblem on it? I wear these types of t-shirts every day. Ask him about his shirt. What about his shoes? You could say something like, "I have a pair of duck boots too, don't you love those?"

Now you have a conversation! This might seem scary at first but the more you make little comments like this, the more you desensitize yourself to doing it and it will feel less and less uncomfortable each time. I love to strike up conversations with people while I'm waiting in line. It's a great way to kill time *and* you get to possibly meet Mr. Right! At the very least, consider it practice time.

WRAPPING UP

Conversation can be a stumbling block for many men and women but if you're prepared and you're paying attention, you shouldn't have any problems advancing things. Just remember:

- Formulate your own opinions about things – now; what kind of food do you like to eat, what's your favorite movie of all time, what one place would you like to visit, etc.
- Watch his body language for cues he's getting bored or excited, adjust accordingly
- Pick up on his cues when he's talking so you can bring up topics he's interested in
- Look at what he is wearing/buying/eating/driving to uncover what he likes

Chapter 7

TALKING LIKE YOU'RE ALREADY IN LOVE

Did you know there is a progression to conversations? As soon as I lay this out for you, you're going to do what I did when I first learned about it – nod your head and say, "Yeah, that sounds about right."

LEVEL 1: SOCIAL

In the first level of conversation, you keep things pretty much on a social level. You probably even throw out a few clichés. "Boy it sure has been hot for September" or "Boy it sure is nice having a pro hockey team in town now." These are what most call superficial topics, topics that anyone can talk about for a few moments. There is nothing to be gained or lost in this conversation. No personal information is being shared. You're not really expressing any deep feelings or opinions. You're feeling each other out to see where it all goes. The problem is you want to have a deeper conversation with a man if you want him to feel he's already in love so you need to advance.

LEVEL 2: FACTS

Once you feel comfortable with someone, you may slide into providing a few facts about yourself. This might include your job or what part of town you live in. You're digging just a little deeper and beginning to share more personal information. In this level of conversation, you'll begin to determine whether or not the two of you have anything in common. You might say you're a diehard Packers fan and he will reciprocate with, "Yeah Aaron Rogers is good but I'm still a Tom Brady kind of guy". Common ground. It doesn't matter that you don't root for the same team, in fact, it adds a little bit of spice to the relationship.

LEVEL 3: PERSONAL

When you reach level 3, things get to a more personal level. You begin to discuss how you feel about things. "I really love it when the leaves begin to turn" or "I really enjoy how quiet and pristine everything is after a good snow". You're sharing things that move you. You're beginning to let him see tiny parts of your soul. No, you're not telling him your deepest desires but you have to get there first. This is a level of sharing feelings that allows you to share without fully exposing yourself. This is the point at which you can for sure have a healthy debate on a topic and feel secure in doing so. That quarterback conversation in level 2 now turns into some friendly banter, "I bet Brady throws for more yards this season than Rogers!" or "Yeah well we'll see you in the Super Bowl pal!" with a smile thrown in for good measure of course!

LEVEL 4: "WE"

In level 4, you've reached the deepest level of conversation. Not only are you sharing very personal details about yourselves, but you're also using "we" statements now, not "I". "If there is snow on the ground this weekend, 'we' can maybe go snowboarding" or "I thought 'we' could go to the store Saturday morning to get some snacks for Sunday football watching". You're implying that you're a couple by referring to yourselves as 'we'.

A great example of "we" is not even using the word! You can kiddingly refer to him as your boyfriend or husband to the bartender or waiter. "I will have the lobster bisque and my husband will have the clam chowder." Then you can laugh hard! This sets the stage for him feeling that he is already in a committed relationship even if it's the first date. It's even better when you just met and someone asks about the two of you.

GREAT, NOW WHAT?

It's okay to slip in some personal and "we" level statements. Don't do this right off the bat, obviously, but as you two get to talking. This might not happen on a first meeting but you should be able to slip it in soon after. Let's envision you're on a first 'official' date after you picked him up at the charity event last Friday. In the course of conversation, you let something personal slip, something like, "Boy I'd love to be one of those women who can just get up and run out the door but if I don't wash my hair every morning…whew it's a wreck!" Now, that might seem silly and certainly whatever you say needs to follow the topic at hand, but play along. Now, Adonis might come back with something like, "Yeah ever since I shaved my head, I've been able to get up and out pretty quickly. I never realized how much work hair was until I didn't have any!" This will probably be followed with laughter, which is always a good thing.

Another thing you might try is slipping in a "we" from time to time. "Hey if it's not pouring next weekend, I thought maybe 'we' could go hike that trail you were telling me about last week" or "I thought after dinner 'we' could take a walk around the park".

By sneaking in and out of level 3 and 4 conversations, harmlessly, you're beginning to treat your relationship as if it's farther along than it is. Of course, you don't want to share all of your personal details and you don't want to assume "we" need to do everything together, but slip one or two in during the course of the date and watch him warm up even more!

SHARE CAREFULLY

While it can be endearing to share with someone that your one flaw is that you bite your nails or you once stepped in a tray of paint and got paint all over the carpet, it can be off-putting if you share things which are too dramatic. For example, "I got arrested for running topless across the park" is probably not as endearing as stepping in a tray of paint. "I had to apply to 6 dental schools before I found one willing to take me" is not endearing while "I cried like a baby when my pet parakeet died" is. Know what to share and what to save for later.

A NOTE ON LISTENING

Nothing is worse than sharing something personal about yourself, only to find out the other person isn't listening. Listening is one of the most difficult skills to learn and many of us, men in particular, are terrible at it. Most of the time, especially if we're trying to impress someone, we are only half listening. The other half is trying to 'top' what they've said or come up with a similar story to share.

Listening takes effort but it is really a common courtesy. When we listen to someone, we hear the cues I mentioned in the last chapter. We can begin to show empathy when it's required and we can respond in kind. By listening, we are telling the other person, "Hey, what you're saying is important to me and you have my undivided attention!" How many times have you sat in someone's office, trying to have a conversation with them, only to sit there watching them scroll through email or write down things that have nothing to do with your conversation. When you catch yourself thinking of what to say, stop and tune back in.

ACTIVITY #9: LISTEN

We are all bad listeners so you're activity is to start working on being a better listener. When you catch yourself in a conversation trying to figure out what to say next, stop yourself and just listen. The words will come, if any are needed. Don't try to 'one-up' or top the story you just heard. You don't need to be sadder, more miserable, better or more unique than the person you're talking to. This won't impress them, it will scream "I lack confidence so I have to feel more important in this conversation than you". Lose-lose situation!

WRAPPING UP

- Don't hang out in level 1 conversation for very long; at least advance to level 2 and begin sharing a few details about yourself, once you're comfortable of course

- When you share things he may find 'cute', he's likely to share back; be able to respond appropriately and let him know what he shared is okay

- Use level 3 and 4 conversational tidbits from time to time to make him believe he's in love with you already

- Share personal details carefully; you don't want to scare someone off with off-putting details about yourself

- Remember to be a better listener than you are a talker; listening shows your interest in what he's saying

Chapter 8

SHARING YOUR STORY

Remember way back in the beginning of this book when I said that each time you leave your house, you should go prepared to find love? Well it's time now to circle back to that again.

ALWAYS BE PREPARED

Let's imagine you're at a party your friend Becky is hosting. She's invited some people from work and a few folks from your mutual circle of friends. You're lingering around the crab dip when Adonis walks up. You'd spotted him earlier and flashed him your big smile, followed by a few quick gazes and here he is. He might open it up with something like, "Boy Becky sure throws a great party" and your reply would, of course, be the standard, "Yeah she loves having her home full of people". After a little more small talk (level 1), he may say something like, "So what do *you* do for a living? I haven't seen you around the office. (level 2)".

This is your opening. You now know he works in the same office as Becky and maybe you've even heard her talk about Adonis before, but even if you haven't, you now know how to respond. First of all, it's important to remember that men love confident women so your answer needs to ooze with confidence. Secondly, you need to love your job, even if you currently hate it. Nobody wants to talk to a Debbie Downer. You may sense this guy is into powerful women so you want to make your job sound as important as you can.

Also, remember to give him something to grab onto and reply with. Don't just say, "I'm a secretary" or "I'm a dentist" or whatever. Say, "I work as an attorney with a small law firm here in town. We handle cases involving medical claims against doctors. We represent the doctors. We have a really interesting case right now where…" Now, you've given him something to grab onto. He can ask questions about what you do and you can have an intelligent conversation. If you just say, "I'm an attorney", there isn't anywhere to go with that. It just lies there, flat on the ground, waiting on someone to pick up the conversation again. Chances are, it'll just lie there and he will move on.

ACTIVITY #10

Know how to answer the 'basic' questions like, "What do you do?" or "What's your favorite type of music"? Have several answers prepared and practice them. I know it seems silly, but you don't want to stumble over your words when it counts. Obviously you won't exactly know your audience but you know where you hang out and what your friends are like. You can guess that a friend of a friend will be similar.

KNOW YOUR AUDIENCE

If you grew up in New York City, for someone else who grew up in a big city, you could share how you couldn't wait to leave the hustle and bustle of big city life. If you're talking to someone who loves art, you might say something like "New York City is great if you want to spend a day just wandering a gallery or two. Have you been to the …?"

When you tailor your story to the person you're speaking to, you immediately bring them into the conversation on a topic they're interested in. Let's say Becky gave you a head's up that Adonis just got a promotion. You can say something like, "I'm working toward a promotion in my firm. Right now, I'm a Junior Partner but I'm hoping to make Senior Partner in a few months". This gives him an opening to share his promotion, about which you can be extremely excited!

Try to throw out some topics you know he'll like, based on what you've been able to figure out so far. If he's a complete stranger, you might have to do some intense listening but with time, you'll know just what to say.

Remember, not all of these tips are meant for the first time you meet. Of course, "What do you do for a living" is bound to be a first meeting question, but these conversational skills are not just meant for one date.

A NOTE ON CONFIDENCE

Men like confident women. I mentioned that above. As you start sharing your story, you need to be sure you're putting that confidence out there. A man will look past appearance if a woman exudes confidence. The problem is, the more relationships we get into and out of, the more hits our confidence takes. Before you know it, you can be a high-power, confident career woman with low-power confidence when it comes to dating. This sums up a lot of my coaching clients. I know you're a very intelligent, successful woman but that doesn't mean you don't struggle with dating. You're not alone.

If you feel your confidence isn't where you'd like it to be, you can start with my confidence-building book, *Comfortable in Your Own Shoes*. This book is a great first step to building your confidence. For other helpful tools on building yourself, you should visit the "Build Yourself and He Will Come" page on my website.

WRAPPING UP

- Be prepared to share who you are and what you're about
- Have more than one version of "your story" prepared to fit multiple opportunities to share
- Don't be a Debbie Downer, like your job even if you currently hate it
- Men like confident women, if yours needs a boost, get to work on it now while you're still reading!

Chapter 9
HE NEEDS TO EARN A DATE

I've mentioned this previously, but it's important for you to remember. Men love to chase. More importantly, they want to know they've earned their way into your life. I always tell women who are in *dating mode* to get busy first.

WHAT DOES IT MEAN TO GET BUSY?
No, I'm not talking about hopping in the sack. By *getting busy* I mean I want you to find things to occupy your time. I want you to develop hobbies if you don't have any. Hobbies are things that keep your hands and mind occupied. Good hobbies might include photography, baking, sewing or something similar.

I also want you to be passionate about something. Do you love animals? Do you love art or music? Are you passionate about helping kids with Autism or working with underprivileged? Are you passionate about politics or victim's rights? Find something you can be passionate about and get involved.

Getting busy also means taking classes or joining MeetUp groups that are doing things you're interested in. Maybe you enjoy old movies – find a MeetUp or local group doing the same. If you're interested in baking or cooking, take some classes to hone your skills.

Why do all of this? I thought you'd never ask!

When you have hobbies and passions, not only are you more interesting, but when a guy calls at 5:00 on a Friday night, expecting you to be free, you can say, "I'm sorry, Adonis, I'm busy tonight but I'd love to meet you for lunch tomorrow if you're free." You should be careful using this when you're first being asked out by Adonis. If you put him off the first time he asks, he may not call back. Being busy, or what some might call *playing hard to get* is a tool to be used sparingly. You don't need to use it every time and you want to be excited to hear from him the first few times he calls.

I know, in some of my other books I've told you putting a guy off is okay, and it is but there are things to know. For one, if a man thinks you're being pursued by multiple men but he is *the chosen one*, at least for that date, he will like you more – *a lot more*. This doesn't mean you say, "Well, Adonis, I've already gotten a call from Charlie and John and Steve but for you, baby, I'm available."

No. But, this is where being busy can come into play. Let's say you've gone out with Adonis maybe 3 times now. He calls at 4:30 on a Friday afternoon. You can *be busy* Friday night and it shouldn't turn him off, especially if you make an accommodation in your schedule for him soon thereafter. You don't need to tell him you're going to book club or cooking class. "I'm sorry, Adonis, but I've got plans tonight. How about we do something…." and you sub in your time.

You've now planted the seed that there *could be* other men angling for your attention but **you're still interested in him.** If you *are* dating other men, only subtly hint at this. You don't actually need to tell him there are other men – the suggestion in his mind is enough.

WRITE YOUR STORY

As I mentioned, hobbies and passions help you have an interesting story to tell. I'm all about building your story. Your story is what you've experienced in your life, where you've gone, what you've seen or heard and what interests you. It might be how you spent the summer with your family as missionaries in South America or how you've spent the last year learning how to give vaccines to different types of animals so you can volunteer at shelters. Maybe it's how you traveled to Europe or have tried every beer in a local beer tour. Whatever it is, it's what makes you mysterious and interesting to Adonis. It gives you things to share about yourself. It gives you things to talk about. It gives you an opinion about things and it makes you more confident – everything Adonis seeks in a woman!

But Gregg, I don't *have* a story!

ACTIVITY #11: WRITE YOUR STORY

You probably do and your next activity is to write your story as it is today. Your story will be different, depending on how old you are. If you're in your twenties, your story will center around childhood and teen experiences. If you're a woman in your 30's or 40's, your story may be more about travel, career or other types of experiences. If you're older yet, you've probably got a really great story.

Dig into your past. Where have you gone? What have you studied? What types of events or causes have you volunteered with? What concerts have you attended? Have you met anyone famous? Have you done something unique or exciting like bungee jumping or sky diving? Do you love to ski or kayak? Whatever it is, it's *your* story and it makes you unique. Write it up. If your story feels like it's a little too boring, let's work to create a new and exciting story – it is never too late! You should always be adding new chapters! Do this before you start dating!

Once you've written your story, look for ways in which you can add to it. Write a bucket list. What would you like to do in the coming years?

WRAPPING UP

- Get busy in life so you have interesting things going on around you
- Uncover your passions and hobbies to keep yourself busy
- Don't play hard to get right off with a man, it will put him off
- Write your story and write what your future story is, then go after it

Chapter 10
THE BEST FIRST DATE

You might think a great first date is dinner or drinks. It's so common it's cliché. Science has proven us wrong, yet again on this one. While dinner is a nice way to sit and talk and enjoy one another's company, if you're trying to stir feelings of love from a man, it's not going to get you anywhere.

HEIGHTEN THE EMOTION

In one study, researchers took men to a scenic area where there were two bridges to walk across. One bridge was pretty sturdy and the other swayed like crazy when you walked across it. At the end of each bridge, a female research assistant presented the men with the task of writing a brief story about their experience. After the men turned in their story, the research assistants gave the men their phone numbers and casually mentioned that the man could call if he wanted to *further discuss his experience.*

The men who went across the solid bridge wrote more 'bland' stories while the men who had walked across the swaying bridge wrote the sexiest stories. The men who had walked across the swaying bridge were also more likely to call the female assistants to *further discuss their experiences.*

Now, having said that, you don't need to go bungee jumping on a first date to get him to fall in love with you, although that's certainly an option. I would suggest something a little tamer like horseback riding, surfing, kayaking or even a walk after a snow when things are quiet and it's a more emotional experience. If you aren't into action, it's perfectly acceptable to go for something emotionally exhausting like a scary movie, a concert by his favorite band, a ballet (if you can get him to go) or even a moving play. If you can find out what tweaks his buttons, you can suggest something like that. Maybe he's into classical music – you can suggest an outing to a classical music event or to the opera. Think in terms of what will get his emotions up or what will make him feel a tad anxious.

In another study, some males were told they would be getting an electric shock that would hurt a bit while others were told it would barely be noticeable. They were then introduced to a female researcher they thought was also going to participate in the experiment. Subsequently, they were asked to fill out a questionnaire about the woman. Those who thought they were going to experience pain rated the female more favorably than those who were told the pain would be minimal, if any.

What is happening here is that, once again, you are stimulating those fight or flight hormones, the PEA, in his brain. This is the same thing we talked about with the eye gaze in the beginning. You're just transferring this from a first meeting to a first date.

ACTIVITY #12: KNOW YOUR TOWN

It's difficult to suggest a fun date or one which will heighten the emotion if you don't know much about your town. Whether you're in a small town or a big city, you need to know what's available. Where are the closest bowling alleys? Where can you go for a great hike, to go kayaking or to enjoy a great band? What sports teams are in your town? Where can you go for the best burger, Italian or Greek food? Start checking out these places so you can honestly say, "There's a great burger joint just around the corner from All Star Bowling".

WE'RE REALLY THE SAME

While women are verbal, men are action-oriented. This shows up in love in all kinds of ways. Men will do things to show they're in love while women will say the words, *I love you*. Women often get frustrated when a man won't say *I love you* and they miss the cues that he truly is in love. Let's transfer this to a first date.

I just suggested to you that you offer up an adventurous or emotionally stirring experience with your man. You're scratching your head thinking, *but Gregg, I want to **talk** to him and get to **know** him on a deeper level.*

Yeah, I get it, but let's read my first paragraph again. Men like action.

To that end, if you don't want to take him on the first type of date I suggested, take him on a date doing something *he* enjoys. If he's a huge basketball fan, offer up going to a game as a date. If he's a hockey fan, go to a hockey game or football or whatever. It doesn't need to be sports either. Maybe he's into old cars or airplanes. Suggest going somewhere where you can look at some old cars or check out airplanes.

What's important here is that you're showing interest in something he likes. Even if you don't know the first thing about basketball, you can get him to believe you do and that you have a similar interest. If you truly do have a similar interest even better. You might even be able to combine two of your interests. For example, if you're into photography and he loves old cars, you can take your camera along and photo him next to some of his favorites.

Whatever you do, your goal is to let him believe you share an interest – that you're similar in that way. More importantly, you're accomplishing this by *doing things* together, not talking. The last thing most men want to do is sit across from you and have a 3-hour feelings talk over appetizers, dinner and dessert. You say "Let's go bowling tonight" and he's there with bells on!

Can the two of you have dinner together? Sure, but if you want him to fall in love with you, you're better off to help him know that you're interested in what he's interested in so he will see how well you fit into his life.

WHEN DINING OUT

If your date does include dinner somewhere, make it somewhere that won't break the bank. The last thing you want is for a new man in your life to think you're only into him for his money. How do you do this?

You suggest a *quaint little place* for dinner. Translate quaint little place into nice but not expensive. Don't suggest the $50/plate steak joint in the heart of Expensiveville. Suggest the little hole-in-the-wall Italian place with great lasagna or the cute little burger joint just down from the bowling alley. I know you want to go somewhere fancy but save that date for a special occasion and a time later on when he knows for sure you're not just looking for a sugar daddy.

LET HIM BE A GUY

Let's face it, nobody is perfect, least of all men. Some men are perfect gentlemen and were raised to hold out the chair for a lady, take her coat, etc. but some men weren't. It's also possible to fart or spill wine. Regardless of your man's flaws, for heaven's sake don't make a big deal out of them.

Chances are he's trying really hard to impress you and he had absolutely *no* intention of embarrassing himself with gas or clumsiness. Let things go. If you really like this guy, you can subtly work on his manners later. If you make a joke or even kindly dismiss what happened, his feelings for you will immediately decline. Allow him his little screw-ups, after all, he is just human!

WHAT TO WEAR

I know, I know. You're already stressing over what to wear on a first date and you haven't even met the guy yet. Women amaze me this way, and I grew up with 3 older sisters! Let me clue you in. He won't notice what you're wearing if he's attracted to you. He'll be too busy imagining what you look like without all of those clothes on. Stop stressing over clothes. I know I said earlier that he might remember later, but what I'm saying is that clothes isn't how you impress him.

By the same token, again, cut him some slack. Men are usually clueless about clothes. Not all of them but many of them. He didn't give 5 minutes of thought to what he pulled out – and he should have. He pulled out the first thing he saw that wasn't: walking to the laundry basket by itself; wrinkled past recognition; stained from last week's pizza after work; or smelling like the soccer field. That probably left him with very few options. Men don't know a thing about 'black belt means black shoes' so don't cut him down to size for it. Men don't always understand why it's wrong to put on a stripe shirt with plaid shorts or something similar. It's clean, it smells good – take what you can get.

Now, what you do want to pay attention to is your hair, makeup, nails and your smile. Remember before I said red or pink lipstick! Men are much more tuned into these details than what you're wearing.

WRAPPING UP

- Suggest a first date that stirs up his anxiety and he will have some truly warm and fuzzy feelings for you after
- Suggest a date where you're doing or exploring something he loves and he'll begin to see you fitting neatly into his life
- Let him be a guy and ignore his foibles and faux pas
- Don't get all stirred up over attire – he's clueless to both yours and his
- Do make sure you've got your hair and makeup done (remember-natural not piles of makeup!)
- Always smile…never forget to smile

Chapter 11
WE'RE SO (UN)ALIKE

Let's say you are doing all the right things to meet your guy. You've given yourself choice and comparison. It has come down to two candidates. The first is a complete opposite of you and other is very much the same as you.

They both get you excited so which should you choose?

When considering a long-term relationship with someone, we want to find someone who has similar values and beliefs as our own, but we also want someone who will stretch us a bit. This seems counter-intuitive but it's not, really.

Imagine if you married your identical twin. You liked all of the exact same foods, all of the exact same sports, all of the exact politicians, etc. Everything the same. How long would it take you to get bored? How long would it take him to get bored? The answer on both accounts is about 5 minutes.

The science says choose someone who is very much the same as you. "Birds of a feather flock together." All the studies point to picking a suitor who has similar interests, morals, beliefs and outlooks on life. Similarities bring comfort when the times are tough. Similarities make us feel secure.

Basically, if a man perceives you as being similar to him, he will feel a stronger connection with you.[2] This makes sense if you think about it. If you are a homebody and he is to, weekends gel. So does rock climbing in Yosemite, if that's an activity you both enjoy.

SORT OF SIMILAR

The ideal relationship has just enough same to make things comfortable with some different thrown in for adventure. What this means is that you do want him to see that you fit neatly into his life, but you also want to be different enough from him for him to be intrigued by you and want to learn more.

Let's go back to Adonis. Our boy loves football and baseball. He grew up in a small town and he still lives there. He enjoys rock music and he's never met a plate of spaghetti with meatballs that he didn't like. Now, along comes Julia. Julia played lacrosse in high school and was an army brat who lived all over the world. She settled down in the same town as Adonis because she got a job there after graduating from a university nearby. She's also into Italian and loves music, but she's into jazz.

---

2. Donn Byrne. *The Attraction Paradigm*, 1971.

On a first date, Adonis and Julia might first grab a quick dinner at the local Mom and Pop Italian place before heading out to a concert. Julia knows the lead singer of a jazz band so she suggests they head there after dinner. This is a great first date because they're doing something they both enjoy – having Italian for dinner – and they're attending a concert. Adonis is open-minded enough to try the jazz concert and finds out he loves it so all in all, it was a great night!

Adonis got his food-love stirred up, which is always a good thing, but he wasn't forced into an evening of the usual first date conversation. Since they both love Italian and they're in a Mom and Pop type place, there are probably some great local icons there they can discuss. At the concert, they get to have fun and just enjoy the music. The pressure is off to spend too much time talking, which puts the fear of God into most men anyway. Adonis now translates having a great evening and doing things he loves with Julia. Win-win.

Your important takeaway here is that minor differences can be complimentary qualities which help one or both of you grow as individuals. The question we must address right now is *how can you use this information to help a guy fall for you*? Look for men who are similar to you. Of course, you won't know if you are similar until you go out on a date or two. Your best tools are coming up. Some are overt and some are covert, but they all work!

TALK ALIKE

In America, we all speak basically the same kind of English. Sure, in the south, there are different accents than up here in Boston or out in California but generally speaking, we speak the same language. Still, there are nuances. Some come based on where you grew up, others on your socio-economic status, others still on your career.

I know I'm dating myself here but let's look at the later seasons of M*A*S*H. Remember Major Charles Emerson Winchester III? He was a *Hah-vaad* graduate from *Bah-ston* who was really affluent and spoke with that hoity-toity tone most of the rest of the world hates. Just by the way he talked, the writers of the show were able to indicate that he came from a higher socioeconomic class than his tent mates. Mimicking his language is a covert, or subliminal tool you can use.

When you are dating someone, you want to create similarity in your language. This isn't to say you fake a southern accent if you don't have one – please don't, but you can utilize some of the clichés or figures of speech he's using. A great example is how people refer to children.

Let's say your guy says "Yeah I have kids." You don't want to come back with, "Oh really, how old are your children?" He's using "kids" to refer to his children. You want to mirror his language. You might come back with, "That's great. I have three kids myself" not "I have three children". Use his language. It helps him feel connected to you in a way he can't explain.

I owned a chalet in Campton New Hampshire. I spent months renovating it on the weekends. If a woman referred to it as a cabin I would be bummed. A cabin, to me, is a one room shack with an outhouse whereas a chalet evokes a beautiful home in the Swiss Alps. It would behoove a woman who liked me to say chalet and not cabin.

In New England, if you call a young woman ma'am, it's insulting. It means an older woman. Miss is the proper word to use here.

Speaking his language makes you an insider. Calling his construction job, his gig could be off-putting unless he said it first. That's why listening is so important on first dates. Listen to the words he uses to describe his life and use his words even if they are not yours.

BEING CLASS CONSCIOUS

Are you aware that different types of people move differently? Different classes move differently. Have you ever gone to a polo match and watched the folks move around? Do you think they move like people tailgating at an Ohio State football game? Nope.

People are most comfortable within their own class of people. It's not me being mean – it's just fact. I would not be comfortable at a biker event because I'm not a biker. I also would not be comfortable going out with a woman from royalty because that's too hoity-toity for me. Fanning my face and wearing a bow tie would make me run! I'm more of a farting, shorts wearing, type of guy!

If you feel similarities and you want to draw him in, study how he moves. Does he take his time sitting down at the restaurant? Does he slide into the booth and smile like I do because I think it's fun? If my date slides in and laughs, I would really like that! If she scrunches up her face and looks at me as immature, guess what? Check please!

If you want to target and attract a man of higher socioeconomic status than yourself, you need to learn the mannerisms, behaviors and language of that type of person. You're not going to marry a Charles Emerson Winchester III if you say, "Ain't that a pur-ty flower yon-ways"? He probably wouldn't even know what you're saying. You would want to say something more 'affluent'.

Additionally, if your guy is Charles, you wouldn't want to flop down on his mother's sofa. You would want to gently bend at the knees first, sit down toward the front of the sofa and glide back. Conversely, if you're eyeing Adonis, who grew up in the blue collar part of town, you could probably flop down on his mother's sofa and she wouldn't think a thing of it. I'm not trying to stereotype here at all. Maybe Adonis' mom came from old money and would stare you out of her living room for such behavior. My point is this – know your audience and talk/behave in like kind or forget about Mr. Right.

If you really want to marry up or down, spend some time watching movies or TV shows that depict where you're headed and learn the language and mannerisms before you set your sights on a Charles.

ACTIVITY #13: KNOW WHERE YOU WANT TO GO

If you really want to date in a different socioeconomic class from your own, whether that's up or down, learn the language and mannerisms of that group. Watch movies, begin to hang out where they hang out and learn the nuances to how they speak and move. Begin to practice these things so you will better fit in when you meet your man.

WRAPPING UP

- Your ongoing goal is to create at least the feeling of similarity between you and your targeted man
- Learn his likes and dislikes and highlight where you are similar and compatibly different
- Use similar language to his to make yourself feel like you're part of his group, not an outsider
- If you want to find a guy of different socioeconomic status or culture, learn the mannerisms and other attributes of that group so you can mirror them

Chapter 12
THREE CRUCIAL WAYS TO BE SIMILAR

There are three areas in which you and your man need to be similar in order for a truly long-lasting relationship to happen. They will reveal themselves, each in due time, in a relationship. They are interests, beliefs and what a relationship should or should not be. Let's deconstruct each of these so you know what to look for and what to do.

SIMILAR INTERESTS

In some of my books, I talk about why men get spooked in a relationship. I get emails every day from women who have been with a man for a few weeks, months or even years and then, out of what seems to be out of the blue, he bolts, leaving her wondering what happened. He got spooked. Plain and simple. Why? This is actually pretty simple.

Men get spooked for three main reasons: (https://www.whoholdsthecardsnow.com/yourtango-the-experts-why-do-men-get-spooked/)

- He fears you're a gold-digger

- He's afraid you'll make him stop seeing his friends
- He suddenly realizes he'll never have sex with another woman – ever again

When you and your man have similar interests, this mitigates the second fear. If he can go to the bar and watch football with you tagging along (and enjoying it), he's good. When the girlfriend and the guy friends get along, his world gets a lot easier. This is why it's so important for you to find this common ground early on. Remember, men are action-oriented. He will not find love for you in long, romantic talks. He will find them in the activities you do together.

When he expresses something of passion to him, if you want him to fall in love with you, don't dismiss it.

Adonis: "Did you see that they're playing old Hitchcock films this weekend?"

You: "Oh. Yeah."

The air just went out of his tires. He was excited about this Hitchcock film fest but you just seemed bored with it. Try again:

Adonis: "Did you see that they're playing old Hitchcock films this weekend?"

You: "Yes! I did, I was hoping to catch a few of them!"

Now, Adonis feels a newfound kinship to you – old Hitchcock movies. He's feeling a little warmer and a little fuzzier about you right now! With the first scenario, it's pretty much game over.

I know what you're thinking. Gregg, do I really need to fake it like this? No. If you don't want to date Adonis, don't bother to show interest in Hitchcock but if Adonis is your dream guy you might want to seem excited about Hitchcock.

You need to pick your battles. Besides, have you ever seen an old Hitchcock film? Maybe you will enjoy it. The other side of this battle is that if you are so agreeable to something he loves, he's more likely to be open to something new you might suggest.

SIMILAR BELIEFS

This one is markedly more important to women than it is to men but the truth is that if you have different beliefs, you will have discourse in your relationship sooner or later. It isn't important that you share all beliefs, but it is important that you share a couple of important ones.

For example, I'm a big cat person. BIG cat person. If I were with a woman and the subject of cats came up, I would either be turned onto her more or off of her based on how she would respond to, say, a cat in need. I had a friend who watched a cat being tossed out of a moving car once. My friend stopped and picked up the cat and took her home. She's now the family pet. Let's turn this into a dating situation.

Let's imagine you and Adonis are on your way to that Hitchcock film fest. The next film begins in 20 minutes and you're about 18 minutes out. Suddenly, you watch a cat being tossed out a car window. Adonis, remembering that you mentioned your work as a volunteer at the local shelter, immediately stops the car and runs across the road to rescue the stunned cat. You are going to feel all kinds of warm and fuzzy for Adonis because he shared your love of cats.

Listen to him and pay attention to the things he finds important. These hints can come from anywhere. He could mention volunteering or something his family 'always did' or any number of things. Keep your radar up and dialed in. When the opportunity to show him you have similar beliefs comes along, jump on it and let him know you're right there with him in what he believes.

The good news is that you can do this without conversing over a topic. Let's remember our 5 steps from Dr. Perper. Step 5 was synchronicity. If he's talking about a pet hamster who drowned in the basement utility sink, slump your shoulders in sadness. If he gets excited talking about his pet Labrador, Stew, who can catch a Frisbee from any distance, show excitement and amazement at the appropriate times. Mirror his emotions. This creates that last step of the process. The good news is that, most of the time, you have a split second or three to observe how he reacts to something so you can react accordingly.

SIMILAR ATTITUDES ABOUT LOVE & RELATIONSHIPS

This is a conversation many couples never have, and it's often the problem that comes between them. Why don't people go here? Partly I think because they don't realize they need to and partly out of fear. If you find the similarities in interests and beliefs, it's difficult to imagine you could have different viewpoints about love and relationships and yet, it happens all too often.

People also don't want to have a perceived *difficult* conversation for fear of scaring off the other person. There certainly is a right and wrong time to have *the talk* about love and relationships, and better sooner than later, but then again, not too soon either. Confused? Okay let's dissect.

For some people, a healthy relationship is one where you each maintain a lot of independence, maybe even living in different cities, but you spend small bursts of quality time together. For others, they want to be with their partner every night and want to share many aspects of their lives together.

What is imperative is that you each come to understand what the other person views as too much intimacy or not enough. What is too much independence versus not enough? Too late in relationships, people find out that they aren't compatible in these areas or they fail to recognize the way in which their partner views relationships.

In relationships, we tend to be pretty selfish at times. We want our partner to love us how we expect to be loved, but we often don't take the time to learn how *they* want to be loved. The longer our own needs go unmet, the less we care about the other person's needs and it spirals out of control. The trick is that if you ask this type of question of a man too early, he will freak out but if you wait too long, you could be too deeply invested. Either one could end painfully.

So what to do?

The best way to approach this is hypothetically and not until you've reached an appropriate level of intimacy with a man. I can't tell you when that is, but what I can tell you is that this isn't first, second, third or even 10th date stuff. You'll know. What you want to do is present it as a hypothetical question or as if you're asking for someone else.

You: Adonis, my nephew asked me a question but I'm kind of stuck on just how to answer. Can you help me?

Adonis: Sure, what's the question?

You: Well, he was asking me what an ideal love relationship would be and I wasn't sure how to answer him. What advice do you think I should give him?

Your next job is to listen and engrave this in your mind. What he tells you is *his* ideal love relationship. It's at this point that you must be honest and determine whether or not his ideal fits with yours. Let's look at an example:

Mark and Mandy have been dating for a couple of years. They met through mutual friends at a charity work event. Over the course of their dating, they've uncovered many similar interests and they share a love of animals and sports. Mark's parents were divorced and both remarried, spending little time with Mark as he grew up. Mandy's parents have been married for almost 30 years. They are home bodies, doting on their two grandchildren, Mandy's nieces, and spending time working in their yard.

Mark's view of the ideal love relationship is one where you give each other some space. Travel is important to him and he doesn't really have close family relationships because he isn't truly close to either of his parents. Mandy, on the other hand, is very close to her parents and her sister. Her ideal love relationship is a close-knit family who is kind of in each other's business but she sees this as normal. She doesn't understand when Mark doesn't want to share every little detail of his day with her and she's often hurt by what she perceives as coolness on his part. Mark is beginning to feel smothered by her constant need to know everything.

If they simply talked about what the ideal love relationship is with one another, they might be able to sort it out. Mark might come to understand where she's coming from and vice versa. However, they're headed down a collision course at this point because their views are so different. There is hope for them if they can talk it out and come to some sort of middle ground, but if they don't, it won't end well.

BUT HOW?

This one is tricky, but you can pick up cues as you go along. People inadvertently divulge these little snippets of their lives as they talk with you. Mark may have said something like, "I was never really close to either of my parents growing up. They both kind of did their own thing after their divorce and just passed me back and forth." An astute Mandy might have taken note that he doesn't have experience with the same type of close family relationship she has and maybe notched it back a little bit.

I've said it before but it's worth repeating. In forming a love relationship, you must become a better listener than you are a talker. You must be always looking for cues and tips on what the other person is trying to tell you, purposefully or not. And when those cues come, you must suck them in and file them away. Ignoring such important cues will come back to bite you some day.

THIS SEEMS LIKE A LOT OF WORK

This is a lot of work, but if you want a solid, loving relationship with the man of your dreams, it's not going to be easy. I never promised easy. Just the roadmap. You're going to need to do some work and so will he. The great thing about relationships is they tend to be automatically reciprocal most of the time. If you show an interest in one of his passions, he's likely to take an interest in one of yours. If you take note of his needs and wants in a relationship, he will probably do the same. A good man, a high value man, will go the extra mile to do the same learning and listening you're doing.

WRAPPING UP

- There are three areas of similarity necessary for a successful relationship: interests, beliefs and ideal love relationship; don't skip the last one

- Similar interests is something you develop as you get to know one another and meanwhile, you fake it a little or try to mingle one of your interests with one of his to create a new one for both of you

- Similar beliefs will be uncovered as the relationship grows; look for cues and try to show him you share beliefs

- Similar ideas of what love relationships are is where couples fail but it's vital to a successful relationship – again, look for cues and be aware if there are great differences so you can communicate to sort them out

Chapter 13
YOU...COMPLETE ME

You might think I'm gonna talk about the movie *Jerry McGuire* here, but I'm not. I'm going to go back further in history to another movie, *Rocky*. Somewhere in the movie, Paulie is asking Rocky why he likes Paulie's sister, Adrienne. Rocky says "We fill each other's gaps". Whether it's "you complete me" or "we fill each other's gaps", it means the same thing. You have enough in common with someone to like one another and enjoy one another's company but there are things about both of you that are different. Adrienne was smarter but Rocky had the street smarts. She was the sensible one, he was the dreamer. Gaps. One brought the other back to earth.

In a relationship, as I've said before, you want to have similarities but you want those differences too. The trick is that the differences can't come between you. You can both be politically different if you allow one another your own opinions and don't stick your nose into their voting habits. You can both root for opposing sports teams if you keep it fun and light-hearted. If, however, politics is your life, you might not be able to overlook this difference. If you get a paycheck from the Browns but your boyfriend is a Ravens fan, you might have a problem. It's all in how much weight you give to those differences.

HOW DO YOU UNEARTH WHAT'S IMPORTANT TO HIM?

You might be wondering how you learn what he can live with. Good question. This stuff can get tricky fast! You unearth this by asking questions about past relationships. This is, of course, conversational material for later in your relationship.

You can ask questions like "What clicked between you and Mandy" or "What was the one thing she did that drove you nuts?" Even "Why did you break up" is a fair question if your relationship isn't too young. You want to have this conversation, of course, when things between you two are good. You could start by sharing your own experience. "You know, when Bob and I broke up, it was his constant need to know where I was". Then you can gauge how your man responds, "Yeah, I hate it when someone is smothering like that. Sara was that way"… and so you go on.

ACCENTUATE THE POSITIVE

Once you know what your man likes or dislikes, you can go back, a couple weeks later, and make sure he knows where you excel. If he had a smothering girlfriend previously, give him plenty of space. Don't bug him about where he is when you're not together. Even if it's driving you crazy, let it lie. If he wants to share it with you, he will. Besides, if he's out with his buddies, you should be doing your own thing. We'll talk more about this a little later.

What you want to be careful of here is not to make a big deal out of being different and you definitely don't want to accentuate your differences before he's gotten comfortable with the similarities. You're doing a fine dance here and you're going to need to trust your gut for some of these things, but I have faith in you.

If you're a confident woman, this will all come naturally. You may be starting to break out in a sweat thinking this is all too much to handle and remember but really, it's not. In all honesty, a lot of this is repetition. We've spent a lot of these last chapters talking about the same thing, just digging a little deeper each time. That's how your relationship will go. You'll begin on the surface and slowly, steadily, dig just a little bit deeper into the next layer until you reach the core, which is where you've found success.

WRAPPING UP

- You want to have differences between you or you'll get bored with one another
- Find those differences by asking questions about his past relationships – but not too soon in your relationship
- When you uncover those things other women have done to undo a relationship, take note and make sure to be the opposite or as close to it as you can be
- After a couple of weeks have passed, you can take those little things that bug him and make sure he realizes you're not that girl
- Accentuating your differences should come only after he is secure in the similarities you share – he should know you're similar in interests and beliefs before you begin pointing out where your differences lie

Chapter 14

DON'T MAKE A MAN YOUR HOBBY

Before we go on, I think it's important to take a brief interlude to cover this topic. If you've read any of my other books, you may have seen this before but it's so important that I want to make sure you see it.

WHAT IS MAKING A MAN YOUR HOBBY?

If I had a nickel for every woman I've asked, "What hobbies do you have?" and gotten the response, "Well, I used to enjoy ….. but then I met Jerry and I stopped…", I wouldn't need to work!

Earlier, I emphasized writing your story. In this, I included that you need to have hobbies and things about which you're passionate. What I left out of *that* conversation that I'm going to tell you now is this – don't give up those hobbies and passions when you meet Adonis. In fact, it's crucial that you keep them.

Making a man your hobby is the equivalent to:

- Doting on him too much
- Being in his business too much
- Always worrying about where he is or what he's doing
- Whining about him not spending enough time with you
- Not allowing him to have guy or even alone time

This will drive a man away as fast as the 3 reasons men get spooked.

HOW TO AVOID MAKING HIM YOUR HOBBY

In order to keep from making him your hobby, keep yours. If you still haven't listened to me and you don't have hobbies, it's time to find some. Hobbies are things that, at the very least, consume your thoughts and I believe they should also occupy your hands.

When he wants to go watch Monday Night Football with his buddies, a woman without hobbies will say, "But Adonis, I wanted to spend tonight talking". Adonis just felt his balls retreat.

What you want to say instead is, "Great! I've got plans with Katie and Sara to go to a cooking class tonight! You guys have fun!" Now, he's excited on two fronts. Not only are you condoning his guy time but, he might get a tasty meal out of the deal soon. Win-win.

Hobbies keep you busy. They help you refocus your energy away from doting on him. This will have a wonderful effect on his psyche – it keeps his feeling of independence. It also allows him to miss you. All **great** things to keep the relationship healthy!

OTHER BENEFITS OF HOBBIES

Hobbies also make you mysterious and interesting. They add to your story. If you come home from an evening art class with a painting you completed, a high value man will likely say something like, "Wow, Babe, that's awesome". Meanwhile, you've become a little more mysterious to him because he saw something new and interesting about you. What other talents do you have?

Without asking me, my girlfriend came home once with 2 shelter cats. I walked in and the 2 kitties came running up to me in full purr mode! She was babysitting for a week because our shelter was full. The very fact that she did this on her own was something I really liked because it surprised me. I asked myself, "What else is this woman capable of?"

Of course we kept both of them…Gizmo and Tucker.

Hobbies keep you busy too. Being busy keeps you out of his business and gives you someplace to retreat to when you're stressed or feeling lonely. Rather than dump your stress on him or nag him to *come be with you* in your loneliness, you can bury yourself in painting, photography or who knows what.

Hobbies can also help you build intimacy with your man. If he has a hobby you can join in or vice versa, you begin to share moments together – memorable moments. This also works if you can combine hobbies, as I mentioned earlier. I call this putting *Pennies in the Jar* and its foolproof when it comes to building your relationship.

ACTIVITY #14: HOBBIES

You probably predicted this but it's time to find a hobby. If you have one, find another one. Two is fine, three is okay too. What's important is that you have things you can occupy your time with when you need to. You need things to add to your story, things to go to when your man wants to hang with his buddies and things to do to keep you busy.

WRAPPING UP

- Hobbies help you keep your relationship humming by keeping you from becoming a nagging girlfriend

- Having a hobby helps you manage times when he wants to be alone or wants to spend time with his guy friends

- Hobbies make you mysterious to him and when he finds you mysterious, you're golden. I got hit with 2 cats!

- You can build intimacy between the two of you by sharing a hobby

Chapter 15

SUPPORT WHO HE THINKS HE IS

Again we're going to dip into soothing the male ego. I know you have an ego which needs to occasionally be stroked as well, but like anything else, if you stroke his, he'll stroke yours.

We each have our own way in which we think we're special or unique. Deep inside, we all want to be known for something. You might want to be known as the best chef in the northern hemisphere or the best at giving massages or maybe you want to be known as someone who is fair and impartial in tense situations. There are endless possibilities.

Men are the same way. Your man wants to excel at something. There is something about himself that he wants you to recognize in him and he wants others to see it too. He wants to be *known*, at least among his close-knit circle, for this special quality. Your job is to find out what this is and then, subtly stroke his ego. Luckily for you, I can lay out a four-step dance you can perform to make this all happen without him knowing a thing!

STEP 1: HE'S CAPTIVATING

We've talked and talked already about being interested in him – showing him you are interested in what he's got going. You now want to take it a step further, without being ridiculous. Let him know you're absolutely captivated by him.

You can do this by listening when he talks about something about which he's passionate. You can further the feeling of captivation by mirroring his emotions as he speaks. He's excited – you're excited. He's sad – you're sad. Show enthusiasm when he's talking about his passion topic. If you don't, he will feel really hurt.

STEP 2: SHOW EMPATHY

Empathy means you show him you understand how he feels. You've felt his pain. You've experienced the joy he describes. You've suffered the loss he's explaining. Whatever it is, you need to mirror the emotion.

Empathy isn't sympathy. "Oh I'm so sorry your Mom died when you were 12." That's sympathy. That's the standard line most people deliver when they really **don't** care.

"I understand. When I was 14, my dad was seriously injured in a car crash. While we didn't lose him, it was touch and go for a while. It was a terrible time in my life." That's empathy. This shows him that you not only do you care, but you can relate directly to his feelings and this draws him to you.

STEP 3: THE IMPLIED COMPLIMENT

Now, it's time to be smooth. You can deliver a compliment in such a way that it doesn't come off as forced or fake and it's barely noticeable but yet it makes the recipient feel really good.

"Wow, Adonis, you really know your way around a carburetor" or "Adonis, I had no idea you were so athletic". Implied compliments come in the form of "Wow your prowess in this area surprises me". This is not forced and you shouldn't sound fake saying it. Be real. "Adonis, those ribs are the best I've ever tasted. You really know how to grill 'em up right!" One of the best ones goes like this, "Your friends look up to you – you have a gift." This one hits him twofold: It shows him that **you** are impressed and **his friends** are too. You have his attention!

STEP 4: THE COMPLIMENT

The problem you begin to run into with the implied compliment is that they get old. You can only deliver the rib compliment once without it seeming fake. Studies have shown that a direct compliment from a stranger or acquaintance will deliver more pow than an implied compliment from a lover if the relationship is older.

The compliment can be delivered in many ways, depending on how deep into your relationship you are. Let's look at them now.

PRAISE WITH YOUR BODY

No, I'm not talking about sex here. What this involves is allowing your eyes to search his body, dart away and come back as if to do a "wow" double take. Use your body language to deliver cues. This is where your eyes also come into play. Use your gaze, your bedroom eyes and even those "I can't take my eyes off of you" looks to cast your approval and provide that silent compliment.

Also don't forget SOFTEN. Make sure to lean in, nod in agreement and smile. All of these are compliments because they show you're interested in him and what he's saying or doing.

EMPATHY

We just talked about this. You don't have to use complete sentences to indicate empathy. Simply nodding your head or mirroring his facial expressions can signal empathy. The "Mm hmm" or "Uh huh" can also be uttered to flow along with what he's saying. Phrases like, "I would have done the same thing" or "I understand how you feel" or "I can imagine". These all show him you get his pain or excitement.

Let's try empathy.

Adonis: I used to play the guitar but I got so busy with college and then work that I haven't had time for it.

You: That must be frustrating to love something so much and not be able to spend much time on it.

Easy as pie!

Other great phrases might be, "You were right" or "I can relate" or "I see what you mean".

He is trying to impress you and he's trying really hard right now. He feels he must one-up any other man you may be considering. Remember, I said men like competition? Well here we are again in competition mode, an unspoken competition, yes, but competition nonetheless.

What you want to do here is indicate to him that the most minute detail about his life is more interesting than the most fascinating thing about you. He may try to do the same and that's okay. He's playing the game too. Game on!

TAKE NOTE OF MINUTE DETAILS

Just like a great comedian comes back to a same joke, time and time again throughout his routine, you can elicit a happy emotion in your man if you remember some minute detail of his life and bring it up later. This could be something as simple as, "Hey I remember you saying you loved Rice Krispies and I saw they were on sale at the supermarket."

Alternatively, you could try something like this, "Hey Adonis, how did that big meeting go with your clients?" This is something you say the next time you see him after that big meeting. He may not even remember mentioning it but you remembered and now you're taking interest in something important to him. It counts!

HAVE A PRIVATE JOKE

This one won't come easily, but once you have it, you're golden. Listen as he tells stories. At some point, he will have a moment he's particularly proud of or a moment where he *saved the day* in a story. You'll know it when you hear it. Later, come back with this and make it your own private joke. Make sure you pull out a point in the story where he rescued the day or did something especially great or unique to help things along. Don't choose a time when he embarrassed himself.

ADMIRE HIM

Now, I don't want you to get the wrong idea with any of these suggestions. I'm not suggesting you get all fake and wishy-washy. What I'm telling you is these techniques will add to his feeling of love for you. One way to make him feel love toward you is to admire something about him. What we're really talking about here are delivering some kudos.

CHAPTER 15: SUPPORT WHO HE THINKS HE IS

You: Adonis, how did your presentation go yesterday?

Adonis: I'm not sure. I think it went okay but I guess we'll just have to wait and see.

You: I could see how knowledgeable you were on the topic when you were explaining it to me.

Adonis: Yes, I really did a lot of research to make sure the whole thing came off just right.

You: Did you get any early feedback from your boss?

Adonis: He felt it went really well. I got a great compliment from him.

You: It sounds like it was well deserved!

This conversation might seem boring, but you're delivering a few kudos along the way. You want to lead with "I can see you did" or "Sounds like". You can also try shorter phrases like "Good going" or "Great effort" or "Wow what a great idea". Anything that lets him know you think he did something great fits in. The good news is men eat this stuff up.

MORE IMPLIED COMPLIMENTS

Implied compliments are great tools, especially for stroking the male ego. Here are a few more ways to deliver them:

- Anyone as good-looking as you
- A person who's as smart as you are
- Someone as fit as you
- You're so well spoken that
- With your great work ethic
- A man with your intelligence

Keep 'em coming but don't be fake. These are to be used intermittently. Don't sprinkle an entire conversation with them. The key is to launch these salvos here and there. Too much and you take away the positive impact.

PRAISE WHAT HE'S PROUD OF

We've talked a little about this but let's go over it again now. We all have things for which we're proud. Maybe he went back to college while working three jobs and graduated cum laude. Maybe he delivered a presentation and wow'ed the group with his joke opener. Chances are, when he delivered one story or the other, he was more excited and animated. That is the one you want to praise later. We all want people to acknowledge what we've done that we're proud of but not everything noteworthy makes us feel excited. Watch his face when he speaks of his accomplishments. If he is animated and excited, you want to take note of that one and circle back to it later.

CHAPTER 15: *SUPPORT WHO HE THINKS HE IS*

Praise the thing they're excited about, not the one *you* perceive to be the greatest accomplishment.

This is a fun related personal story. Guys praising guys works too - in some circumstances. I just bought a recliner and I have been designing a special table that swings over my chair, providing a place for my computer and then neatly tucks away when I don't need it. After the crap I got for buying an *old man recliner*, my friends started helping me improve my prototype. I was obsessed with this silly table!

They know I am proud of this thing so they bring it up all the time and compliment me on what I perceive to be my engineering marvel. I get excited when they bring it up! This instantly makes me happy just talking about this stupid computer table. Now, they could be screwing with me, but I'm too excited and happy to know if they are or not.

STICK TO THE RECENT PAST

When you're delivering praise, focus on something more recent. A man may spend years working toward being the president of a company but if he bench presses 300 lbs for the first time that morning in his workout, that's probably the one you want to praise, assuming, of course, he delivered it with the required excitement. Something that takes longer to accomplish is less likely to be something he's proud of, as is something people may take for granted.

A man who comes from a home of athletic people might not value praise about his latest athletic accomplishment but if he just told a joke to a tense group of coworkers or clients and broke the ice, he might be super proud.

Back to my example. Do my friends praise me for all the #1 bestsellers I have written and the people I have helped? Nope. They know that is my real job. What excites me right now is this table, which helps me do my real job and that's what they want to talk about because it whips me up into a frenzy.

STEP 5: THE KILLER COMPLIMENT

This is the one that will really make him feel all warm and fuzzy. It's a direct hit but not one he's necessarily expecting. As you're looking at him and listening to him, find that one thing about him that truly wows *you*. It could be the way his eyes dance when he talks about his mother or daughter. It could be that you love his sense of humor or that you think he's really got great teeth. Whatever it is, it's something that will bond the two of you. It's an unexpected observation. It may even end up being about something he feels insecure over, like his teeth or his eyes. You won't know that but still, this type of compliment goes a long way toward building a warm feeling between you.

When you deliver the killer compliment, begin with his name.

"Adonis, I can't believe how wonderfully your face lights up when you talk about your daughter."

"Bob, the way your eyes dance when you talk about hiking makes me want to go out right now for a hike!"

"Steve, the way you smiled when you told that story just warmed my heart."

"Joe, I find you to be the most fascinating person I've ever talked to."

Killer compliments should be used **very sparingly** and they're especially effective if you deliver them as you're parting ways. A good rule of thumb is no more than one killer compliment in a month's time, otherwise it'll come off as fake. One final word on the killer compliment, make sure it is indeed a compliment. Don't compliment a doctor on his bedside manner – compliment him on how well he solved a problem or something more challenging. Don't compliment a singer on how pretty his guitar was, tell him how moved you were with his solo.

WHO NEEDS A COMPLIMENT

If your man is incredibly handsome, complimenting his looks will likely fall flat. He's heard it all before. Someone who is less attractive, however, will be wowed by such a compliment, having heard it relatively few times, if at all.

Still, everyone wants a compliment sometimes. One surefire winner is the knee-jerk compliment. Your incredibly handsome lawyer boyfriend just landed a client several firms had been competing over. Praise is warranted here. "Wow that's great! It's no wonder, considering how well prepared you were for the meeting" or something appropriate. One thing to be sure of is that you aim high enough, but not too high. If your boyfriend thinks his speech was mind-blowing, you saying something like, "Wow, great speech honey" might fall flat. "Adonis! That was the best speech I've ever heard! You knocked their socks off!" would be more appropriate.

LAUGH AT (ALL OF) HIS JOKES

Men pride themselves on being funny, even when they're not. Your job is to laugh first and longest. Don't be fake – everyone will see right through that, but be genuine. Make sure he hears your laughter first, and last. This is a huge ego stroke but one he will really enjoy!

HAVE PET NAMES

This won't come early in a relationship but it will come. Eventually, he will share with you that all of his friends called him something growing up. If he speaks of this with fond memories, you can say something like, "Oh that's great. Do you mind if I call you that?" If, however, he grimaces when he tells you they all called him "stinky" because he got sprayed by a skunk, you probably shouldn't adopt that as your term of endearment for him.

RECEIVING HIS PRAISE & COMPLIMENTS

You didn't think you'd get away without learning how to accept praise and compliments did you? Many people who are low on confidence will poo-poo compliments they receive. This is a big no-no. He has observed something about you that he finds wonderful and he's willing to tell you how he feels. Don't downplay his compliment with "Oh it was nothing" or an unemotional, flat "Thanks".

Instead, say something like, "That's so nice of you to notice" or "Thanks so much for saying that." or "You're right, I do look great in this bikini!"

WRAPPING UP

This was a big chapter, but let's sum it up with a few points:

- Use empathy, compliments and well-timed kudos to let him know you admire something special about him
- Develop private things between you both like a private joke or pet names
- Let him know you're intrigued by him
- Receive his praise and compliments with appropriate enthusiasm, don't let them fall flat
- Use all these techniques sparingly or they will lose their impact

Chapter 16
KEEP THE HOME FIRES BURNING

It's very important that, once you've snagged a man and you've both fallen in love, you keep the love alive. So many couples allow themselves to fall into routines, both in their personal lives and in their work. This makes everything so unexciting and boring.

Men need excitement. Men need mystery and challenge. You, as a couple, need to constantly be putting *Pennies in the Jar*. I've written an entire book on this as you may have guessed. Let's get the nickel tour of how to keep the love burning hot in your relationship.

INTIMACY ISN'T SEX

First and foremost, you need to understand that building intimacy can be done without having sex. Intimate moments are private, personal moments you share between you. It may be that private joke or the pet names you develop for one another. It could be supporting him when his sister dies of breast cancer or helping him prepare for the biggest presentation of his career.

When you build intimate moments between you, you're shoring up the walls of your relationship. You're putting special moments between you that he doesn't want to lose. It's very hard to go into a new relationship and rebuild intimate moments. He wants the moments he's already built with you.

HOW TO BUILD INTIMACY

You can build intimacy in a relationship many ways and not all things you do together will build intimacy but they will all work to keep your relationship hot. For example, if he loves restoring antique cars, you can build memories and intimacy by taking an interest in this hobby. Go to antique car rallies or shows with him. Be there with him as he shows off his baby. Look hot doing it and he'll be extra proud!

You can also build your relationship by noticing his effort around the house, "Adonis, it means a lot to me that you volunteer to do the dishes after dinner." Everyone likes to feel appreciated and men are no exception. "I love how you painted the bathroom walls without getting it on the mirror. Maybe next week we can do the bedroom together?"

Another way to keep from getting bored with one another is to plan date nights. Alternate whose turn it is to plan. You do one week, he does the next and the other person can't complain about the date. If he chooses to go to a hockey game and you don't care for the sport, put on

CHAPTER 16: *KEEP THE HOME FIRES BURNING*

your best sweatshirt anyway and go happily. No groaning allowed. I am a huge fan of the weekly date night, no matter what stage your relationship is in. The more kids you have, the more important date night becomes!

Take a lesson from your early attraction lessons and decide to spend 2 minutes looking into one another's eyes – without laughing or breaking contact. You'd be surprised at how well this works!

Going grocery shopping can actually be fun if you engage your light-hearted side and your boyfriend. Split the list and make a race out of it or make it a scavenger hunt. Give him clues to some of his favorite foods that are on the list then send him on his way to find them. Another way to insert fun into grocery shopping is to each choose three foods you think the other will like or buy all of the ingredients for the other person's favorite meal. Of course, if your man is a novice in the kitchen, he might need some help rounding out the recipe, but give him credit for what he gets.

My girlfriend and I have this thing going where we cannot ever stop our cart in the grocery store – it must stay in motion. Try making a salad without stopping. Yes, I can do it but feel sorry for the guy who needs to clean up after me!

One great thing to do for your relationship is to check in with one another weekly. This is tricky if you don't go into it with an open mind and a loving heart, so make sure you've got both before heading in. One of you starts – maybe it's the one who didn't plan this week's date night, just so you can keep track. Anyway, that person is allowed to speak about how they feel in the relationship at that point in time. They're allowed to share any frustrations or excitement, concerns or kudos they want. The only job of the other person is to listen. You don't get to interrupt with your 'yeah but's' and you don't get to argue while the other person is speaking. Once one person is done, the other can go and the same rules apply. It's a listening only exercise. Once both are done speaking, you can engage in a conversation. With any luck, you both listened without being defensive and you'll have an engaging and positive conversation about how to fix any concerns one or both of you have.

A great thing to do for your relationship is plan a one-day or weekend staycation. During this time, you don't make any plans. You can even tell others you're going away so nobody bothers you. Then, just do whatever you want that day. Go shopping or take a drive. Paint the bedroom or just sit and read. Whatever you do, make it a day together and don't let anyone interject (emergencies excepted of course).

There are many other ways to add pennies to your jar, and you can find them in my book, *Pennies in the Jar: How to Keep a Man for Life*.

LEARN HIS LOVE LANGUAGE

There are five love languages, as defined by Gary Chapman. We often forget about these and we need to be reminded! It is crucial that you uncover your partner's love language. When you speak to him in his love language, he receives the love you're trying to send. If you're oblivious to his love language, his needs will likely go unmet and he will feel unappreciated and unloved. The same goes for you, of course. This could even be an activity you undertake together. "Honey, let's work on figuring out what our love languages are." Make it fun.

AFFIRMATIONS

Some folks want to be verbally appreciated – they want words of affirmation. "Gee Jerry, I love how you mowed the lawn and trimmed around my flowers! It looks great!" If your man loves words of affirmation, he will feel extra special upon hearing these words! I'm a firm believer that even if your love language isn't words of affirmation, we should use them anyway. Everyone wants to be appreciated!

ACTS OF SERVICE

Some folks want you to do things for them, like cook their favorite meal or plan a date at someplace they love. This is all about actions – which most men are into anyway, as I've said many times already. Acts of service can be simple little things like making his lunch for him before he goes to work or helping him prepare for a big presentation. It can be picking up his clothes at the dry cleaners or buying a birthday card for his mom for her birthday. Its little things, not big things that will make the difference.

RECEIVING GIFTS

Now, don't take this to mean you need to go buy him a gold watch one week and a Hugo Boss tie the next. Receiving gifts can be something as simple as putting a note in his computer bag that says, "Knock 'em dead today!" or "Just want you to know I'm thinking of you". Buy his favorite cut of meat at the market or bring him his favorite type of chips for the football watching weekend. Gifts come in all shapes and sizes. Get creative and he'll love you forever! I love Yodels. My girlfriend brings me home Yodels and I'm instantly super happy!

QUALITY TIME

Some folks just want to spend time with you. They simply want your undivided attention for a little while and is that so much to ask really? If your man wants quality time, he will be happy just spending time doing simple things with you. Read to one another or share something great about your day. Give him time to unwind with a glass of wine and a pair of ears. You could just pop some popcorn and watch a movie together. Whatever it is, it's about the time, not the event.

PHYSICAL TOUCH

This one may be the deal breaker for some relationships. If you're with someone who requires physical touch as his love language and it's not yours, you're going to have to dig deep and be very tolerant. You have to remember, it's how he feels loved, not you so you might have to suck it up and deal. I think when two people who both require physical touch end up in a relationship it's a match made in heaven. The other love languages are easier to dish out, even if it's not your cup of tea but some folks don't want to be all touchy-feely and some require it. Be aware if this is his love language so you know whether or not you're willing to go this extra mile!

WRAPPING UP

- It is important to continue working on building your relationship as long as you're in one; there is never a time when you can let things slip to autopilot
- Focus energy at least once a week on spending time together, one-on-one
- Learn his love language – and yours – so you know what you both require of one another

Conclusions

You have, in the clutches of your nicely manicured hands, the keys to making a man fall in love with you. It's like a big magic wand you can use to bring in the man of your dreams. There is no game playing here, there are no mean tricks or underhanded methods. It's all straight science and you now know how to use it.

I love helping women and, as I've mentioned, any man will be clueless to the fact that you wooed him in. He will almost immediately believe he spotted you first and worked his magic on you. Let him have his little fantasy – it doesn't hurt anything and when you're dating, months down the line and people ask, "How did you two meet?" let him tell his story of attracting you. Just smile a knowing smile and let him go.

I've thrown a lot at you here, but you can handle it. There isn't a lot in here about building your confidence and if you've read my books before, you will notice it's missing. That's no accident. Even if your confidence isn't very high, you can set your mind to doing anything I've told you in this book and your confidence will grow.

Anyone you see who is confident in something was first terrified. The first time any 5th grade boy asks a 5th grade girl "out", he's petrified – even the *cool* kid in class. Any time a man finds a woman truly attractive, his knees are jelly as he approaches. If they aren't, consider the possibility he's a player! Good men aren't very practiced at wooing women. This means that, even if you're a little shaky, know he is too.

The good news for you is your part is often silent and sly. Looking a man in the eye is not a verbal or outward action. You just do it. If he looks away and doesn't look back, no harm, no foul. If, however, you catch him looking your way again a few minutes later, you're on to something! Meanwhile, you haven't said a thing. You didn't have to approach, talk or anything. Just look. You have the easy part.

Study what is here but don't feel you have to do everything by the letter. Know and understand the important elements of attracting a man and make yourself comfortable doing them. Begin smiling at strangers – all strangers – and let that build into a more confident action. Smiles always make people feel better! Consider it your effort to making the world a better place!

CONCLUSIONS

Learn how to listen. Practice on family and friends. Begin to listen for cues in what *they* are telling you. You may find out new things about them that you didn't know! Each little thing you do to practice makes you better and better.

Start paying attention to what you look like when you leave your house. I know it's a pain in the butt to put on a nice pair of jeans and a top without spaghetti stains on it, just to go to the grocery store, but you'll kick yourself if Adonis is there and you're in your pajama pants – even *if* you put on the red lipstick!

Once you've caught a great guy, make sure to follow through on not making him your hobby, support who he thinks he is and accentuate the similarities between you. All of these things help him to fall in love with you.

The right man is there for the taking. You now have all of the tools you need to draw him in and make him feel as if you're part of his life already. You have tools other women don't have. Your only job now is to go out there and find him!

Good luck!!

Author Bio

As one of Boston's top dating coaches, my books rest prominently atop the dating advice genre. In my role as a life coach, I've been known to be unorthodox, in a good way, and I break a few rules. I assist both men and women and help them understand one another.

I won't bore you with my professional bio. Instead, I will share with you the story of how I became a dating and life coach and what makes me qualified to coach you.

The irony of my story is that I come from an extremely dysfunctional family. I witnessed the marriage of my parents crumble before my eyes at an early age. Flying dishes seemed normal in my household. I came out a bit angry and I have 12 years of failed relationships to show for it.

Fortunately, I started encountering positive things in my life. I discovered that couple, that elusive, elderly couple still holding hands in the park at the ripe old age of eighty. They gave me hope. As a problem solver, I could solve anything…except relationships, damn it!

I couldn't figure out why my folks represented the norm rather than the exception to married life. Fifty-five percent of all marriages end in divorce. Why? "What is wrong?"

In 2009, after a long stretch of living the single life, I had an epiphany. I attended a Christmas show at my Dad's church. I am not a religious person, but when I saw the cheerful couples and witnessed the powerful music, I was touched. I needed answers to love and I wanted true love for myself.

I was tired of my shallow single life. I decided to study my failures and interview as many single people and couples as I could. I even watched the movie, Hitch, and it motivated me to help others.

I realized I possessed a natural ability to help others discover love, and knew it was my future. Can you guess where I started? Yep, those happy elderly couples. Sure, I got maced a few times as I approached them with questions, but the knowledge I gained was priceless!

Since then, I have met thousands of people: happy couples, unhappy couples, single people of all types, and everything in between. I quickly learned that confidence played a large role in both attracting and keeping a partner.

AUTHOR BIO

My friends encouraged me to launch a dating advice website. I now own the top dating site for women, Who Holds the Cards Now.

Men and women contact me after reading my books. I have become a "Dear Abby" of sorts. Today, after thousands of interviews, I have accomplished my goal. I broke the code and enjoy a great relationship myself. Now I plan to share my findings with **you**!

I have come to realize that even though people believe what I teach, they still suffer a serious problem. They lack the motivation and confidence to execute my tactics. A course change was required. I started concentrating on life coaching in addition to my date coaching. If you can't love yourself, how can you love someone else? It's impossible.

Now, I concentrate on pulling people in and guiding them to understanding themselves. I assist them in creating clarity in their lives, setting goals, and creating the path to attain those goals. I offer inspiration, passion, and spirituality with the constant live like you're dying attitude. People are transformed through my books and daily exercises.

I have written 15 Amazon Best Sellers, four of which reached #1 Best Seller status. Together we can build your confidence, increase your self-esteem, and propel you closer to your goals.

You will discover happiness by completing the work most people will never attempt!

Today, I travel and teach in all the sexy playgrounds: LA, South Beach, and Las Vegas. I can help you in your journey to find love and build confidence so we can transform your life.

I am not merely a best-selling author, my readers are my friends and I communicate with them directly. I humbly ask you to allow me to help you. Join me on my quest for your happiness, your exciting journey to an extraordinary life!

Gregg Michaelsen, Confidence Builder

I feel you need two very important skills before you start dating again: confidence in yourself and an understanding of the male mind. I provide both because I am a life coach and a male dating coach. I have two rockin' paid courses with tons of videos featuring me if you're interested.

Understand men here:
www.whoholdsthecardsnow.com/product/
the-man-whisperer/

Find confidence here:
www.whoholdsthecardsnow.com/product/
build-will-come/

GET THE WORD OUT TO YOUR FRIENDS

If you believe your friends would draw something valuable from this book, I'd be honored if you'd share your thoughts with them. If you feel particularly strong about the contributions this book made to your success, I'd be eternally grateful if you would post a review on Amazon. You can check them out by clicking the links below. My coed motivational books are listed after the women's books.

WOMEN'S DATING ADVICE BOOKS

- Please read the jewel of all my books: *To Date a Man, You Must Understand a Man.* This companion book to all my books will help you understand men! Read the hundreds and hundreds of reviews to learn how well my tactics work! Another #1 best seller.

- Next, take understanding men to another level with *10 Secrets You Need to Know About Men.*

- If you want to make sure you don't get played, you need to read *Weed Out The Users, The Couch Potatoes and the Losers.*

- One of my latest books is selling like crazy! *Pennies in the Jar: How to Keep a Man for Life* is the ultimate women's guide to keeping a relationship strong!

MORE AWESOME BEST SELLERS TO SOLVE YOUR DATING ISSUES!

- If you're single and looking? Read *The Social Tigress*.
- When you can't stand the thought of picking up one more player, you need to read *Weed Out the Losers, The Couch Potatoes and The Losers*.
- Do you want to learn more about men? Read *Manimals: Understanding Different Types of Men and How to Date Them*.
- Are you ready for a serious change? Read *Own Your Tomorrow*.
- Do you want to text a man into submission? #1 Best Seller: *Power Texting Men*.
- Would you like to take yourself on a self-discovery journey? Read *To Date a Man You Must Understand Yourself*.
- Do you want your ex back? I'll give you your best chance with *How to Get Your Ex Back Fast*.
- If you want to regain control of your relationship, try *Who Holds the Cards Now?*.
- Confidence attracts! Get it here: *Comfortable in Your Own Shoes*.
- Would you like to clean up online? Read *Love is in the Mouse* and *Love is in the Mouse 2017*.
- Are you over 40 and getting back into the dating scene? Check out *Middle Aged and Kickin' It*.

- Are you in need of some introvert dating help? Take a peek at *Be Quiet and Date Me!*.
- And, last but not least, for the long distance couple: *Committed to Love, Separated by Distance*.

BOOKS FOR MEN AND WOMEN THAT MOTIVATE!

- *Live Like You're Dying*
- *The Power to Communicate*

I can be reached at Gregg@WhoHoldsTheCardsNow.com.

Please visit my website just for women, WhoHoldstheCardsNow.com.

Facebook: WhoHoldsTheCardsNow
Twitter: @YouHoldTheCards
I'm a Your Tango Expert

You are my motivation!
Gregg

Made in the USA
Coppell, TX
29 October 2019